BEAULIEU
THE FINISHING SCHOOL
FOR SECRET AGENTS

BEAULIEU
THE FINISHING SCHOOL
FOR SECRET AGENTS
1941-1945

by
Cyril Cunningham

Pen & Sword
MILITARY

This book is dedicated to
Lieutenant-Colonel S.H.C. Woolrych O.B.E.
Intelligence Corps
Commandant of the Beaulieu Finishing School

First published in Great Britain in 1998,
reprinted 1998 and again in this format in 2005 by
Pen & Sword Military
An imprint of
Pen & Sword Books Ltd
47 Church Street
Barnsley
South Yorkshire
S70 2AS

ISBN 1 84415 312 6

A CIP catalogue record for this book is
available from the British Library

Printed and bound in England
By CPI UK

Pen & Sword Books Ltd incorporates the Imprints of Pen & Sword Aviation,
Pen & Sword Maritime, Pen & Sword Military, Wharncliffe Local history,
Pen & Sword Select, Pen & Sword Military Classics and Leo Cooper.

For a complete list of Pen & Sword titles please contact
PEN & SWORD BOOKS LIMITED
47 Church Street, Barnsley, South Yorkshire, S70 2AS, England
E-mail: enquiries@pen-and-sword.co.uk
Website: www.pen-and-sword.co.uk

CONTENTS

Until he retired, **Cyril Cunningham** was by profession a Chartered Occupational and Forensic Psychologist. At the height of the Cold War he spent ten years working for various Defence Intelligence departments, was a frequent lecturer at the Army's School of Military Intelligence and was seconded briefly to the Information Research Department of the Foreign Office as an advisor and data analyst.

He left the Civil Service in 1961 to practise as an occupational psychologist in the oil industry but was recalled on several occasions to give evidence on Intelligence matters to a Privy Council committee and other high level Government committees. Later he joined the staff of the Portsmouth Management Centre (now part of Portsmouth University) as its resident senior lecturer in Occupational Psychology and remained there until he retired in 1988.

He was educated at Cambridge University, where he read Law, and Reading University where he obtained an honours degree in Pure Psychology. He joined the Navy in 1943 via Cambridge University Naval Division and was commissioned in the RNVR. He saw active service in Normandy and North West Europe.

He has written many feature articles for commercial magazines and newspapers, including *The Times*, as well as a long list of papers for learned journals including the *Journal of the Royal United Services Institute for Defence Studies*. His book *The Beaulieu River Goes to War* was published by Montagu Ventures in May 1994.

FOREWORD

By

Sir Michael Howard, KT, CBE, MC.
Emeritus Professor of Modern History
Oxford University

In the darkest days of the Second World War, at the end of 1940, the British government established on the Beaulieu estate in the New Forest a very peculiar school indeed. Its curriculum included, among other scarcely less nefarious activities, burglary, forgery, sabotage, slander, blackmail and murder. By the end of the war over three thousand men and women had graduated in some or all of these highly undesirable skills and became agents or officials of the Special Operations Executive. Most of those trained as agents were then infiltrated into the mainland of Europe to inspire and assist the resistance movements in German-occupied territories. About 40% of them were caught by the Nazis, and many of those met terrible ends.

Many books have now been written chronicling the more spectacular of their adventures. M.R.D. Foot has given us an excellent 'official' history of SOE operations in France, and a similar volume has been promised on Yugoslavia, but even these cannot provide detailed and comprehensive accounts of their achievements. Perhaps no such account can now be written, or could ever have been written. Much of the necessary documentary evidence has been lost or destroyed, while even more vital information was never committed to paper. Yet the least that we can do for the memory of these lonely heroes is to ensure that every scrap of information about their activities should be preserved and published, and to this enterprise Mr Cunningham here makes a notable contribution.

As with so many aspects of the British war effort, much of what Mr Cunningham has to tell us is bizarre, verging sometimes on the farcical. Instructors in these arcane but necessary skills were not easy to find – at least, reliable trustworthy instructors. There was an understandable reluctance to recruit on to the staff people who were known to have spent their lives honing their skills at murder, burglary and sabotage, so amateur instructors had to learn as they went along. There was indeed one experienced safe-breaker on the staff, whose presence may remind admirers of Lewis Carroll of the billiard-marker, 'whose skill was immense' on the crew in *The Hunting of the Snark*. There was also a gamekeeper from the Royal Estates who was surprisingly skilled in survival techniques; but the nucleus consisted of handfuls of officers experienced in espionage from the First World War, which included the Commandant, Colonel Stanley Woolrych.

Otherwise the staff consisted of, as one of them put it, "some pretty odd fish". These ranged from, at one extreme, the couturier Sir Hardy Amies and the film critic, scriptwriter and poet Paul Dehn, to the notorious Kim Philby at the other. Philby indeed played a major part at Beaulieu, not only as a memorably effective instructor, but in the foundation of the establishment and as a drafter of its syllabus. To do the old rogue justice, it must be remembered that for most of this period his employers in the Soviet Union were Britain's allies and that he was as keen on the destruction of Nazism as anyone else. He deserves credit at least for the honourable part he played through his contribution at Beaulieu to bringing it about.

As for the students, they were an even odder collection of fish. In addition to the British trainees, there were the even more highly-motivated Frenchmen, Norwegians, Poles and Dutchmen dedicated to the liberation of their own lands. The Dutch were particularly ill-fated: most of them when they landed in Holland found Gestapo reception parties and became victims to the most spectacular German intelligence success of the entire war. The skill and courage of the French had to be balanced against their understandable determination to play the game by their own rules. Finally there was a group of Republican Spaniards, who had been pushed from pillar to post until, as a well known SOE operative put it, "they would cheerfully have killed anyone in the uniform of a British officer". They, needless to say, required especially sensitive handling.

All these groups had to be kept in isolation from one another, and indeed from everyone else. Naturally the purpose if not the very existence of the school had to be kept secret from the local community, which made for additional tensions and difficulties. Readers of another generation may wonder how such an establishment could survive and function at all for so long without being 'blown', but it was by no means exceptional in a wartime Britain in which secrecy was accepted as the norm and people knew that it was unwise to ask awkward questions – let alone publicize the answers.

In the following pages Mr Cunningham gives a wonderfully full account of how Beaulieu functioned; how it was staffed, how it was accommodated, how it was run, what the living conditions were like, what was taught there and by whom, and how the students reacted to the régime. Like the staff of the school themselves, he admits that they could do all too little to prepare their students for the terrible ordeals ahead of them; but the prospect of those ordeals had deterred none of them from volunteering. Most of them were very young, and all were completely inexperienced. Once in the field they would be hunted by ruthless and highly intelligent professionals. They might be prepared for brutality, but all too often they were to underestimate the skill and subtlety of their German interrogators. They also badly overestimated – at least in the early years of the war – the degree of support that they might expect from the population on which their lives depended. It was not all that easy, in 1941–42, to obey Churchill's instructions and 'set Europe ablaze'.

With hindsight it is easy to see, and Mr Cunningham freely admits, the shortcomings of the Beaulieu training. But – again as in *The Hunting of the Snark* – the crew had, at least initially, to depend on a map that was 'a perfect and absolute blank'. They had to learn as they went along. As they gained experience they were able to fill in the blanks, and the disasters of the early years were to be redeemed by a steadily rising rate of success.

The history of SOE is one of lonely sacrifice and ultimate triumph. Mr Cunningham deserves our gratitude for describing how the seeds of the triumph were planted on the banks of the Beaulieu river.

INTRODUCTION
By
Lord Montagu of Beaulieu

In June, 1940, I was enjoying my last term at my prep school, St Peter's Court, which had been evacuated from Broadstairs to Crediton in Devon, and was sitting the Common Entrance Exam for Eton, which I duly passed. But before the Battle of Britain began I was suddenly sent for by my headmaster and told that I was to go home immediately as I was off to Canada. I was excited, but nevertheless sad that I was unable to enjoy my final weeks at school and say goodbye to my many friends.

The aftermath of the surrender of France resulted in many parents making sudden decisions to send their children overseas, as it seemed inevitable that it was only a matter of time before Hitler would invade a largely undefended Britain. My mother's decision was particularly influenced by my stepfather, Captain Edward Pleydell-Bouverie R.N., who had recently returned from France, where, as British Naval Attaché to the French Government, he was responsible for evacuating many of the diplomatic corps from Bordeaux. After seeing the blitz in France himself, he had no doubt that it was advisable to send us abroad. So after two hectic days at Beaulieu and shopping in London, I found myself on the liner *Monarch of Bermuda* sailing out of Liverpool, together with two of my sisters and a governess, and, after an exciting voyage, ended up living and schooling for the next two years in Canada.

When I returned home in September, 1942, Beaulieu was a very different place – the war had imposed itself on the whole area. There were pillboxes hidden in dovecotes, troops everywhere, including the Home Guard, the Navy on the River, but, most important, many of the houses which I knew were out of bounds. As a sixteen-year-old, all this secret activity fascinated me, but most intriguing of all was the talk of what went on in these houses, whose occupants were affectionately known locally as the "Hush Hush Troops". No one was allowed to visit them and friends who had lived there had vanished. What was equally surprising was that the permanent Instructing Staff, some of whom were there throughout the war, and the officers were in the habit of dining with us regularly, playing tennis and attending parties, and the younger ones paying court to my sisters. Consequently, we got to know the Instructors very well, but it was not until V.E. Day that we found out what and whom they were instructing. We also learned that the Germans, as a result of their interrogation of captured SOE agents, knew a great deal about what went on at Beaulieu, and apparently there was a report in Nazi files fully describing my family, including the name of my dog.

After the war I became increasingly interested in recording the contribution that the SOE at Beaulieu had made to the war effort. So I was delighted when Cyril Cunningham accepted my commission to write a book about it and sincerely congratulate him on his comprehensive research and commitment to the task. His previous work, *The Beaulieu River Goes to War*, was equally well researched. Over the years I tried to meet as many SOE personnel as possible – people like Peter and Odette Chrurchill, Sir John Wedgwood, Hardy Amies, Maurice Buckmaster, and particularly Paul Dehn, who wrote the wording on the memorial plaque in Beaulieu cloisters, which I was finally able to persuade the Special Forces Club to support, after some years of frustrating opposition. The day of the unveiling by Major General Sir Colin Gubbins, former head of SOE, brought back many old SOE instructors and pupils from all over Europe, and many laughs and tears graced the occasion as old adventures were recalled and comrades remembered.

All at Beaulieu are proud of how this small Hampshire village played such a vital part in defeating the enemy and giving support and succour to those valiant men and women behind the enemy lines. Thanks to Cyril Cunningham's efforts, this book will ensure that the achievements and courage of Beaulieu's SOE pupils will be remembered for all time.

Montagu of Beaulieu
August 1997

ACKNOWLEDGEMENTS

Foremost among those whom I have to thank is Lord Montagu of Beaulieu who commissioned and sponsored this research, gave me access to his archives, and above all gave me his continuous support and encouragement during the long and disheartening process of seeking a publisher.

I am enormously grateful to Mr. Robert Woolrych and Professor Austin Woolrych, sons of the late Lieutenant-Colonel S.H.C. Woolrych, the Commandant of the Beaulieu Finishing School, without whose generous subvention this book may never have been published. I also have to thank them for information about their father and for permission to use his photographs, the Woolrych Collection in the Intelligence Corps Museum.

My special thanks are also due to Mr Graham Carter of Montagu Ventures Ltd., for much practical help and sterling advice.

I have to thank the following for providing me with substantial amounts of information:-

Mr Gervase Cowell, SOE Adviser, Foreign Office, for information on the School's establishment, curriculum, and an outline description of agent training.

Mrs Ann Sarell (nee Keenlyside) for much information on the School staff and a description of arrangements at The Rings.

Miss Susan Tomkins, Lord Montagu's Archivist, for searching for correspondence between Captain Henry Widnell and the leaseholders of the requisitioned properties, and between Widnell and the Army authorities, including the School's Commandants. Also for providing me with access to the reference library of Montagu Ventures Ltd.

Mr A. Nosak of the Polish Home Army Parachutists Association for supplying photocopies of original documents and for translations.

Mr C.P. Wykeham-Martin for information on the Small Scale Raiding Force and its occupation of Inchmery House.

Mr Gerard Brault for information on Inchmery House and the training of the first RF Section agents.

General George Berge and Madam Berge for information on Inchmery House and Operations Savanna and Josephine B.

Madam Alma Kerjean for putting me in touch with numerous former RF Section agents, and Mr R. Hansford for his unstinting assistance.

Major Richard Shaw, the Curator of the Intelligence Corps Museum, for allowing me access to documents and photographs.

Mr Denis Hendy, who provided much information on the early days of the SOE occupation of The Drokes.

One of my principal sources of information was the former Lieutenant-Colonel Cuthbert Skilbeck, one of the School's first Chief Instructors, to whom I am greatly indebted and with whom I spent a very enjoyable day in February, 1995. Alas, he died in June, 1996.

The following also gave me help:-

Mr Owen Aisher for putting me in touch with Joachim Ronneberg; Miss Vera Atkins, the former Chief Intelligence Officer of the French Section, for putting me in touch with Mrs Sarell; Mr Francis Cammaert, Mr Daniel Cordier, Madam Pearl Cornioly, Mr J. Darton, all former secret agents; Mr Peter Doneaux; Mr Bernard Ettenfield, formerly of Field Security, for his information on the Spaniards at The Drokes; Sir Anthony and Lady Evans for allowing me into The Drokes; Mr John Farmer, former secret agent; Mr H.G. Fleming, formerly Field Security, for his information on the Dutch agents Dorlein and Ubbink; Mr George Jackson for information on Johnny Ramenski; Mr Ivor Kregland of the Norges Hjemmefrontmuseum; Mr R. Lagier, Mr J.J. Landau, Mr. G. Ledoux, former RF Section secret agents; Lieutenant-Colonel Terry Message, Secretary of the Special Forces Club, for putting me in touch with many former agents; Count and Countess Michalowski for allowing me into The House in the Wood; Mr A. Philion for allowing me to visit Inchmery House; the late The Hon. Mrs Pleydell-Bouverie; Mr Joachim Ronneberg, (who led the team of saboteurs that blew up the Norsk Hydro heavy water plant at Vemork); Mrs Decia Stephenson, Archivist of the FANYs; Dr B. Thornton; Mr Jack Trott, Mr Andre Watt, former secret agents.

And finally I wish to thank my sister, Pauline Cunningham, for checking many versions of the manuscript for errors and my wife Mary for her constructive advice on structuring many passages, proof reading, and her support throughout this project.

Prologue

THE PLAQUE IN THE BOOKCASE

On a chilly February afternoon I stood alone in a mood of veneration in the quadrangle within the medieval ruins of Beaulieu Abbey. Before me in the ancient cloister wall was a recess known as the 'Bookcase', where hangs a large, modern, circular plaque which reads:-

> Remember before God
> those men and women of
> the European Resistance
> Movement who were secretly
> trained in Beaulieu to fight
> their lonely battle against Hitler's
> Germany and who, before enter-
> ing Nazi-occupied territory
> here found some measure
> of the peace for which
> they fought.

These words commemorate over 3000 men and women of at least fifteen different European nationalities and a number of Canadians and Americans who, during the Second World War, had been trained as secret agents of various sorts, at what was officially known as the 'Finishing School', a complex of twelve country houses in the Beaulieu area that had been requisitioned by a secret British organization called the Special Operations Executive.

Lord Montagu had asked me to undertake the task of discovering as much as I could about this extraordinary school, which had ceased functioning half a century ago. He knew of me only through my reputation as a local historian and was unaware that I had been an intelligence officer and was uniquely well qualified to carry out the research. In an early phase of my professional career, at the height of the Cold War, I had spent a decade working for a number of intelligence agencies and had actively participated in the training of secret agents. And I had worked with several men, and one or two women, who, during the Second World War, had risked their lives as spies and other kinds of secret agents. I had also worked with spycatchers and had been trained as an interrogator.

The Bookcase is not visible to anybody ambling past the doorway of the cloisters. Visitors to the National Motor Museum, in the grounds of which the abbey ruins stand, must have wondered why a tall, elderly man with grey hair and spectacles, casually dressed and with his hands stuffed for warmth into the pockets of his blouson, was standing bare-headed and shivering in the cold for so long, staring at an ancient wall! But I was shaking, not, as a casual observer may have thought, from the cold, but from the haunting of my private ghosts and the sense of loss and mourning that I felt for all those courageous people I had known whose lives had been packed with high adventure. Most of them had died of old age and their deeds long forgotten but one of them had been shot down while attempting to escape from his tormentors and I had been given the unpleasant duty of investigating the circumstances of his death.

I am by no means alone in being fascinated by the exploits of secret agents. I am particularly interested in what sort of people they are, what traits of personality enables them to stay alive and cope with the enormous strains of leading a double life under the constant threat of exposure. And there is usually a good story in how they came to be agents or how they entered the less hazardous occupation of intelligence officers.

I gathered my wits and began to think about the present. I was acutely aware that Lord Montagu's request had catapulted me back into a business I had left long ago and would impel me to revive my knowledge of techniques that happen to be common to historians as well as intelligence officers. They both have to organize networks of sources and display a wary patience with scraps of information that must be carefully weighed for their validity before searching systematically for their place in a massive jigsaw.

This spot in the tranquil surroundings of the ancient abbey was as good a place as any to gain a glimmer of inspiration as to how I should tackle the task of pursuing a very stale trail and build from scratch a network of sources to provide me with sufficient material for a reasonable history of the school. I was afraid that most of the people who could have enlightened me would now be dead, and if not dead, would be octogenarians with fading memories. As a seasoned researcher I was very much alive to the fallibility of the human memory when trying to recall distant events. I was conscious that gathering thousands of scraps of data is simple compared with the task of piecing it together into a meaningful whole, and I began to wonder if I still retained the knack of spotting the gaps in the fabric and tracing sources and material to make a seamless patch. A smart computer is still no substitute for a sharp eye and an inquisitive brain. I took courage from the fact that at least I had the advantage of some knowledge of the organization and methods of our secret intelligence services, even if I had long since lost touch with my contacts in that business.

My mind was already grappling with the problem of how to convert a catalogue of personalities and events into a form that critics often describe as 'a good read', one which publishers are apt to judge in terms of the number of copies likely to be sold. My instant dread was a publisher who might require his editor to re-work and 'pep up' my manuscript into the modern idiom by transposing events that took place half a century ago into a conversational narration that any half-wit would recognize as an impossible feat of memory on the part of the alleged narrator. The narratives in this book are transcriptions of tape recordings and not figments of my imagination.

On my way home I decided to follow the well-tried research formula of starting by making a systematic search of the literature while simultaneously building a network of people who might be able to help. My first step was to contact the Special Forces Club with a letter of enquiry about SOE training. It produced a response from the Foreign Office and arrived in time to save me from looking, in my ignorance, in the Public Record Office for information on SOE. It was not encouraging. It informed me that 87 per cent of the official records of SOE had been destroyed, that the remaining 13 per cent is buried in the archives of the Foreign Office and is not open to the general public. It said that the SOE Adviser would attempt to answer any questions put to him but made no suggestions as to how one could frame penetrating questions from a basis of utter ignorance. It also stated that the residue of the official records was unlikely to contain very much about the organization and nuts and bolts of agent training. However, I was sent a seven-page handout giving a skeleton outline of the organization of the Finishing School, the names of a few key members of the staff, a broad outline of a few aspects of the syllabus and some information on training problems. Unfortunately it was ambiguous or uninformative on a number of key issues such as exactly what topics were included in the curriculum, and which of them had been taught at which of the schools in the Beaulieu complex, and by whom. And, I was to discover, much of it referred to the situation that had prevailed at the end of the war and did not correspond with eye-witness accounts of what had existed during the earlier years.

When I started my search of the literature, I found that most of the books about SOE had long been removed from the shelves of the public library and had been consigned to a central store and could now only be obtained on payment of a fee, accompanied by an exasperating delay in delivery.

I soon realized that the lack of official records was not, unfortunately, supplemented by the enormous number of books that have been written about SOE. All of them concentrate upon the organization, politics and operations, with brief, if any mention of training. One book, *Specially Employed*, written by Maurice Buckmaster, the former Head of the French Section, which was said to contain valuable information on training, turned out to be very disappointing. It gave only a vague outline of the principles of agent training. Even M.R.D. Foot's official history, which is otherwise very thorough, deals cursorily with the subject of training and is inaccurate in some of the details.

The awkward truth is that there is no authoritative published account of the activities of the British training schools, how they came into being and how they were organized and run. Consequently from the outset my task appeared to be daunting to say the very least. It dawned on me that I had stepped onto a roller-coaster of frustration and elation which would only be endured by a gritty determination to succeed and hopefully a few dollops of downright luck.

As an experienced researcher, I should have expected a bumpy ride in my quest for original data. There were bound to be arid periods when I would make no progress at all after expenditure of immense effort, leaving me with the feeling that I had run up against a brick wall. I ought to have realized, but did not, that there would be unexpected breakthroughs. Sometimes these came by letter and sometimes by phone; in one instance a phone call from the south of France produced a mass of material – in French! But for the most part I acquired data frustratingly slowly, painstakingly, chip by chip, creeping usually towards another dead end and another bout of despair. And on each occasion, just when I had reached the point of abandoning the whole project, another breakthrough would land on the doormat with the morning's post.

While working my way systematically through the personal reminis-

4

cences and biographies of agents who had been caught by the Nazis and had suffered horrible experiences, I found that a high degree of emotional detachment was required in order to examine the facts objectively and carefully to discover whether they had put their training into effect and whether it was effective against routine or stealthy German counter-espionage techniques. Here my experiences as a former intelligence officer and my lifetime of professional knowledge of scrupulous and unscrupulous investigation, interrogation and interviewing techniques proved invaluable.

Most of the British-trained agents took several courses in different establishments; the Beaulieu Finishing School did not have the monopoly of training in certain subjects. Many of the published accounts of training by former agents do not recount with accuracy which particular topics were taught at which schools.

The Special Forces Club put me in touch with a number of survivors who in turn passed my enquiries on to others and brought me into contact with many war heroes and heroines of several nationalities. It was a trail that was to lead to numerous parts of France, to Spain and Norway, to the Norges Hjemmefrontmuseum in Oslo, and to the Polish Stadium Polski Podziemnej in London which sent me photocopies of some very interesting original documents. I also managed to contact such distinguished former members of SOE as the legendary Vera Atkins, formerly the Chief Intelligence Officer of the French Section, now in her eighties, who told me in no uncertain terms that my quest was twenty-five years too late! Nevertheless she put me in touch with an invaluable and generous source of information about the staff and administration of the Beaulieu complex, one of its former secretaries, Mrs Ann Sarrell. Also, thanks to the Special Forces Club, I was able to meet a former Chief Instructor of the Beaulieu training staff, Cuthbert Skilbeck, now sadly dead. I spent many enjoyable hours in his company.

Some former secret agents who survived the horrors of the Nazi concentration camps did not wish to be reminded of their wartime experiences. Others have long forgotten the details of their stay in Beaulieu, or, if they recollected significant events, were quite unable to pinpoint them in time.

At a very early stage of my research I discovered that wartime security measures in the Beaulieu area were so tightly enforced that people living on the doorsteps of the houses requisitioned by SOE had no idea of what was going on in them. The trainees living in the SOE houses were forbidden to talk about their activities and were forbidden to wander outside the bounds of their schools, though some of them did. Field

Security personnel were sent into the nearby villages and especially into local pubs to monitor the conversations of members of the School staff and seek out and return erring students to their houses.

Most of the agents who were trained at Beaulieu are now unable to identify in which of the houses they had been trained, because the houses bore no names during the war years and because the agents were usually transported in and out of them in trucks that had their rear canvas flaps strapped down so that nobody could see who or what was being transported, curtailing the passengers' view of their whereabouts. Nor could they remember, with a few exceptions, the names of those who had tutored them.

It was with misplaced hope of obtaining information from residents in the New Forest area that I appeared on the Richard Cartridge show on Radio Solent and made an appeal for information from anybody who had any recollections of the Beaulieu School. The response was, as I should have anticipated, very disheartening. Only one person contacted me.

After more than a year of probing and prodding, when I had accumulated a substantial amount of data and had already made some key surmises, the Foreign Office came up with information about the School's organization. They had been unaware they possessed it and had found it tucked into the records of another school, STS 17 at Brickendonbury. It included a list of all the topics that had been taught at Beaulieu, but they were unable to name which instructors had taught which subjects. They also discovered the manuscript of the Commandant's Opening Address to new students, and I was able positively to identify the author as Lieutenant-Colonel Woolrych; the alterations were in his distinctive handwriting, which I had come to know well through examining documents that he bequeathed to the Intelligence Corps Museum and by reading his correspondence with Captain Widnell, the Montagu estate's land agent.

Despite the expenditure of a great deal of time on the tedious task of combing through a large number of books, talking to survivors and painstaking research, there remains a shortage of data on recruitment and training policy, who taught what and where at particular periods of the war, who made the assessments of the trainees and how the assessments were made.

I cannot therefore guarantee the veracity of everything that I have written. I have done my best with the material available.

Chapter I

THE SILENT SISTERS AND THE HOYDEN

How do you begin to describe to the descendants of the wartime generation the scale of the calamity, the immensity of the atrocities and the extent of the destruction inflicted upon the world by Nazi Germany over a period of ten years? There are no words to express the magnitude of the evil and the havoc caused by the Third Reich, a nation of seventy million people, when it plunged the entire world into a war that was ultimately to consume the lives of forty million people and devastate most of Europe.

With the exception of Sweden, Switzerland, Spain and Portugal, the whole of mainland Europe including much of Russia was conquered or annexed by Nazi Germany, and four hundred million people were held in brutal subjugation until liberated by the Allied Armies in 1944/5.

The German conquest of Europe began in 1935, two years after Adolf Hitler and his gang of murderous opportunists seized power in the German Republic. By the summer of 1942 the German empire stretched from the shores of North Africa to the Arctic and from the English Channel to the doorsteps of Turkey, Persia (Iran) and the Caspian Sea. In North Africa the British Forces had been driven out of Libya and German armies were entrenched in Egypt poised to strike towards Cairo and the Nile, forming the southern arm of a huge threatening pincer movement aimed at linking up with the German forces in Russia through Asia Minor.

The demands which these conquests made upon German industries, materials and manpower could not be met from its own resources and it ruthlessly plundered the occupied countries to support its war against the free world. The savagery with which it went about this task defies belief. Millions of able-bodied men and women were rounded up and consigned to forced labour in Germany or to slave labour camps and millions of the less able-bodied and those sections of the populations considered to be racially inferior, such as gypsies and jews, were put to death. The peoples of the more industrialized nations like Czechoslovakia and France were made to harness their industries to the production of implements of war, and their agriculture was plundered to feed the German forces.

Those nations that made alliances with Nazism to avoid military conquest, such as Hungary and Bulgaria, were, like the subject nations of ancient Rome, compelled to raise armies to supplement the Nazi hordes in far-away provinces of the Nazi empire and provide oil and other essentials to the Nazi war effort.

The hardships caused to the occupied countries by the diversion of their human and material resources aroused bitter resentment, but fearful retribution awaited dissenters and anybody attempting any form of resistance. The culprits, and often their entire families, were murdered and, as a warning, disproportionate numbers of innocent hostages were rounded up and slaughtered. The scale of the Nazis' systematic slaughter of the peoples of Europe beggars description. Twelve million were murdered. Millions of them were consigned to gas chambers and their corpses cremated in ovens. Apart from the name Auschwitz, kept permanently alive by international Jewry, the world may soon forget the names of numerous other factories of death. Who, now, among the younger generation, will find any significance in the names of Belsen, where 100,000 people died, where the British liberating forces found 10,000 unburied bodies and 13,000 people died after their liberation? Or the names Buchenwald, Dachau, Mauthausen, Ravensbrück, Sachsenhausen and Treblinka, where millions of Europeans, including many British, perished by execution or from beatings, overwork and deliberate starvation, systematic neglect and disease? Miraculously, seven hundred thousand of the inmates of these camps survived.

To these astronomical figures must be added the war casualties among the opposing armies and casualties among the civilian populations, many of whom had the misfortune to live in the path of the conquering and liberating armies.

Small wonder that the savagery of the German Occupation drove an enormous number of people of many nationalities to risk their lives by overt or covert acts of defiance or resistance, despite appalling risks to themselves and their families. A huge number ran away to remote or wooded areas to avoid being rounded up for forced or slave labour in Germany and lived as outlaws.

A great many of those who remained at home embarked upon hazardous enterprises aimed at preserving their national identities, or at succouring and harbouring the hunted and the oppressed, or undertook aggressive and often suicidal clandestine activities against the common enemy. However, individual and unco-ordinated acts of defiance had no more than nuisance value unless they could be co-ordinated, directed at suitable targets and provided with the means of inflicting significant damage to the Nazi war effort.

The governments of many of the conquered countries had fled into exile in Britain and had left behind networks of citizens and agents to keep them informed of events in their native countries. But each country was acting individually, possessed few and tenuous means for maintaining contact with their homelands and only slender, if any, trained personnel and resources at home or in exile for inflicting substantial damage to the occupying Germans.

Britain, standing alone against Hitler's armies after the fall of France in 1940, was ill-prepared for subversive warfare, and its citizens are not conspiratorial by nature. We have no recent history of centuries of oppression and underground resistance like the Poles or the people of other Baltic and Balkan states, no natural aptitude for covert activities and conspiracies, no experience of the dire necessity of mistrusting our nearest neighbours, no knowledge of clandestine ways of establishing the reliability of like-minded dissidents or of how to organize them into clandestine cells.

Until the 1930s the British Establishment abhorred underhanded diplomatic and military practices, and possessed no organizations, as did Hitler's Germany, for arming and encouraging dissident groups, using commando and geurrilla tactics, black propaganda and sabotage and other means of 'underhanded' warfare.

On 7 March, 1936, the Nazis tore up the twenty-five-year-old Treaty of Versailles, imposed on them at the end of the 1914–18 war to prevent them from re-arming, and sent their troops to repossess the Rhineland, the traditional industrial heartland of Germany, removed by the Treaty to prevent them re-arming.

Two years later, in 1938, Germany occupied Austria and the Sudetenland on the Czechoslovakian border, adding ten million Austrians and Sudeten Germans to the native German population and tipping the balance of manpower in their favour over the populations of Britain and France.

Although it was evident to most British citizens that a war with Germany seemed inevitable, the politicians, conscious of the appalling slaughter of the previous World War, were wedded to a policy of

9

appeasing Hitler, a policy that led to their humiliation at Munich in 1938.

Until mid-December, 1938, the British Government was being advised by our Secret Intelligence Service, the SIS, that Hitler's ambitions lay in the East, namely in the Russian Ukraine, despite the fact that they had been warned to the contrary by no less an authority than Admiral Canaris, the Chief of German Military Intelligence, the Abwehr. Indeed, between September, 1938, and May, 1939, Whitehall received no fewer than twenty warnings from a variety of secret sources about the impending aggression by the Axis powers, Germany and Italy. Most of these warnings, intended to stiffen the resolve of Britain and France to take firm action to curb Hitler's ambitions, had been brushed aside by our politicians as Intelligence plants!

Not until the Nazis over-ran Czechoslovakia in March, 1939, did the British Military High Command take any notice of the proposals of a few far-sighted individual army officers, buried in the bowels of the War Office where, since 1935, they had been studying guerrilla warfare and covert offensive action against future enemies. One of these officers was J.F.C. Holland of the Royal Engineers who had been a pilot in the Royal Flying Corps and had fought with Lawrence of Arabia in the First World War. Another, working separately, was Colin Gubbins, a small wiry major in the Royal Artillery, born in Japan, widely travelled, fluent in French and German, and with more than a smattering of Russian, who also had a distinguished record in the First World War and its aftermath, the civil wars in Russia and Ireland. He and another officer, Millis Jefferis, an explosive expert of the Royal Engineers, had produced a *Handbook for Partisan Leaders* and a booklet on the use of explosives for sabotage in guerrilla warfare. By the time war was declared, Gubbins had already personally reconnoitred the Danube valley and the Baltic states looking for likely strategic targets and targets of opportunity and had made contacts within the Polish Intelligence community.

On 3 September, 1939, the Germans attacked Poland, and Britain and France declared war on Germany. The same day two very small Intelligence sections of the War Office, which included Holland's and Gubbins', were combined and started work organizing several kinds of secret warfare and 'stay behind' parties, and various plans had been put into action. Early in the war translations of Gubbins' pamphlets setting out the principles of guerrilla warfare were scattered by air over many countries in occupied Europe.

On 10 May, 1940, the 'phoney war' ended when the Germans launched their blitzkrieg offensive into Holland and Belgium and in sixteen days routed the French and British armies. On the same day Winston Churchill became Prime Minister.

On 16 July Churchill authorized the creation of a department dealing with subversion, sabotage and irregular warfare, to be called the Special Operations Executive. It was controlled by the Ministry of Economic Warfare which was headed by a Labour politician, Hugh Dalton, and was formed by amalgamating three different organizations.

One of these was Section D (D for Destruction) of the Secret Intelligence Service. The Secret Intelligence Service, the SIS, has been this country's main Intelligence and espionage service nominally under the control of the Foreign Office, whose duties have been described by one wag as 'lying and spying'! The SIS is also known as MI6, and its very existence was officially denied until very recent times.

Section D of the SIS was created shortly before the outbreak of the war, a foundling of the Foreign Office which, with characteristic hypocrisy, had authorized the birth while disowning it and any direct interest in 'disreputable' forms of warfare such as guerrilla activities and sabotage.

Section D was headed by Lieutenant-Colonel L.D. Grand and had on its staff a man by the name of Guy Burgess, who was already working for the Russians as a spy! The professed aim of Section D was to stir up resistance to the Germans in Europe by acts of sabotage. Before the war it had been starved of funds and as a consequence it comprised a group of people sitting in a conference room discussing ideas such as how to interrupt Hitler's oil supplies and how to cripple German food production by launching incendiary balloons to set light to grain fields! However, at the outbreak of war it did manage to pull off a few coups, one of which was to evacuate the entire stock of industrial diamonds in Amsterdam before the Germans overran the place!

As far as this narrative is concerned, it was Section D that provided the Special Operations Executive with a nucleus of secret servicemen, and, although they were not from the mainstream of the SIS, they were to be influential in formulating the agent training programme.

Another unit of the triumvirate from which the Special Operations Executive was created was yet another Foreign Office foundling, a not so secret offshoot that had been studying the production of subversive, corrupting propaganda. It was funded by a newspaper magnate and manned by some very well known Fleet Street feature writers and reporters.

The third component comprised several very small Intelligence sections of the War Office already involved with secret warfare, including those

11

of Holland and Gubbins. None of these officers were career Intelligence officers, but were on secondment from their regiments. The professional Intelligence Corps, founded during the First World War, had been disbanded in the 1920s and had not yet been re-formed.

This new secret organization, the Special Operations Executive, or SOE as it came to be called, was to join the ranks of a number of existing or burgeoning secret services, but unlike the others, which depended for their success on lying low and keeping very quiet and unnoticed, this new creation was a hoyden, a rowdy child designed to make its presence felt by causing havoc, and therefore guaranteed to stir up hornets' nests of Nazi counter-espionage and counter-revolutionary agencies. Consequently its objectives were totally incompatible with its sisters, the Secret Intelligence Service, the Radio (monitoring) Security Service (now called GCHQ), and a brand new secret service coming into being to rescue civilians and servicemen from behind enemy lines, MI 9.

The fourth truly secret service, MI 5, the country's main counter-espionage agency, was not so directly affected by the overseas activities of the new organization, and it was soon to provide considerable assistance, in various ways, to the new organization.

The bitter conflict of interests between the SIS and the SOE resulted in a struggle for power that lasted throughout the war. It began by the SIS insisting on keeping control of secret signal traffic, refusing to allow SOE to use its existing training facilities or to impart knowledge of, or allow SOE to interrupt or hazard, its own operations. SOE was therefore compelled to be dependent on its own internal resources which included a nucleus of SIS men, almost all of whom, as we shall see, were as inexperienced in the arts and trade crafts of underground warfare as any of the other officers in SOE. They all had to learn virtually from scratch how to organize, train and control secret agents, and the arts of secret communications, clandestine operating methods and methods of infiltrating agents into enemy territory and recovering them. They were thus compelled to design the syllabuses of their various courses and recruit people capable of teaching a variety of topics, including murder, blackmail, forgery, arson, sabotage and other activities which in normal times would have been regarded as criminal.

Inevitably, as the war progressed, the work of the five main Intelligence services and several other Intelligence agencies overlapped, and also got in each other's ways. One author has estimated that in France alone no fewer than twenty agencies of various nationalities were operating simultaneously. However, it is not the aim of this book to delve into the complicated rivalries and politics of the various agencies and their effects on wartime operations. These have been chronicled in much detail by several British and Continental historians.

The new organization started off badly and within months the Foreign Office political and propaganda warfare component was hived off to a different department of the controlling ministry, the Ministry of Economic Warfare. However, the idea of training secret agents in the art of so-called 'Black' propaganda was retained by SOE and was to be incorporated into its agent training syllabus.

The Headquarters of SOE was housed in Baker Street in London and was headed by Sir Frank Nelson, a former Indian Army specialist in Intelligence, who had with him the nucleus of men from Section D of the SIS and regular army officers seconded to Military Intelligence. This nucleus, acting on the advice provided in the 1922 edition of the *Manual of Military Intelligence*, recruited many leading businessmen, journalists and lawyers with foreign language skills to man the headquarters and its outstations and training establishments. The organization was divided into a number of Country Sections, one of which, the East European Section, was under the command of one of the original War Office team of pre-war researchers, Colin Gubbins, soon to be promoted to the rank of Brigadier and made head of Operations and Training.

The number of Country Sections expanded rapidly to include, in addition to the Eastern European Section, separate sections for Holland, France, Belgium and the Scandanavian and Balkan countries. For our purposes we need only note that the Country Sections were almost autonomous and many were answerable directly to their Governments in exile. For example, the Poles, Czechoslovakians, Dutch and Norwegians had governments in exile which exerted a major influence on operations in their respective countries, though all of them were ultimately dependent on the British and later the Americans for most of their transport and supplies and much of their training facilities.

One of the largest of the Country Sections, that of the French, had no government in exile. The Free French were led by a junior General, Charles de Gaulle, who was not universally recognized as the spokesman of France, either in occupied France or elsewhere, and certainly not by the Americans, who, after the Allied landings in North Africa, were backing another French general, General Giraud.

The result, for our purposes, was that there were two organizations dealing with the training and operation of secret agents in France, the British-controlled French Section, and the Gaullist Secret Service, known as the *Bureau Central de Renseignements et d'Action*, (Central Bureau for Intelligence and Action), otherwise known as the BCRA. To link the two organizations, SOE created a liaison section, manned jointly by British and French personnel, and called it the RF Section. The French Section was to be headed by Colonel Maurice Buckmaster, and the French BCRA was headed by a man who called himself Colonel Passy, whose real name was André Dewavrin, originally of the French Deuxième Bureau, the equivalent of our SIS. And the RF Section was headed originally by a British officer, Captain Eric Piquet-Wicks.

Here again was another conflict of interests, particularly political interests. Although the Free French BCRA was beholden to the British for some training facilities, the transportation of agents, and for a time, all of its supplies, once the agents were in France they could act as they pleased and in their own political interests, especially Gaullist interests.

The reason for mentioning the distinctions between the French Section of SOE, the RF Section and the Free French BCRA is that all three of these organizations used secret establishments in the Beaulieu area, and for administrative purposes were part of the Beaulieu SOE complex.

By the end of 1940 SOE had created a number of establishments for training servicemen of several nationalities in a variety of commando techniques. It retained a close association with numerous commando groups all over the world throughout the war, and often used them for its own nefarious purposes. The commando training of prospective secret agents was to develop into a tiered system, beginning with gruesome physical training and weapons training lasting between two and four weeks and designed to weed out those lacking the stomach and stamina for aggressive action. One such school was based at Wanborough Manor, near Guildford, and another, for Free French servicemen, was based at Inchmery House, overlooking the estuary of the Beaulieu river.

Those who survived the rigours of these courses were sent on parachute courses either before or after special training in close and unarmed combat, fieldcraft, boat work, elementary morse code, demolition training and learning to live off the land. This sort of course was originally designed for the training of commandos and took place at Lochailort, in Scotland, but towards the end of 1940, SOE had set up its own school, known as the MI (i.e. Military Intelligence) Wing, nearby, at Arisaig on the wild north-west coast of Scotland. This school was commanded by Lieutenant-Colonel J.W. Munn of the Royal Artillery, who was destined to become the first Commandant of the new school for secret agents at Beaulieu. Included in the curriculum of the MI Wing at

Arisaig was the deadly art of 'silent killing' with and without weapons, elementary sabotage and the use of enemy weaponry.

In parallel with the development of the commando training schools, Section D of the SIS created at the end of 1940 or thereabouts, a school for training foreign saboteurs. Known as Station 17 or STS (Special Training School) 17, it was located at Brickendonbury Hall in Hertfordshire.

The idea for this school is said to have come from Guy Burgess, who was an established official of the Foreign Office and a member of Section D. In the summer of 1940 he had participated in the recruitment of Kim Philby into his section at a salary of £600 per annum. Burgess had been Philby's secret courier when Philby had been spying for the Russians in Spain in 1937.

According to Philby, the idea of creating a school for training secret agents in the techniques of underground work was first raised by Burgess in July, 1940; Philby said he found it astonishing that such a school did not exist already. (It probably did, but the SIS evidently kept it secret even from its own people and especially from Section D to stop it passing on its knowledge to an outfit like SOE.) Having launched the idea, Burgess left Philby to work out the details, and Philby claims to have been the architect of the syllabus, the system of agent selection and the type of accommodation required for the school.

Philby's proposals were put to a Section D training committee and after some discussion and an unknown amount of modification led to the creation of Station 17, the SIS sabotage school for foreign trainee agents at Brickendonbury Hall, a former school standing in spacious grounds near Hertford. It was at this school that a team of Norwegians was trained to sabotage the German heavy water production at the Norsk Hydro plant in the Norwegian province of Telemark, and where the Czechs trained to assassinate the German SS chief, Reinhard Heydrich, 'the butcher of Prague'. This school was initially placed under the command of a naval officer, Commander F.T. Peters RN, later to earn a posthumous Victoria Cross for gallantry during the Anglo-American assault on Oran harbour in November, 1942. He had survived the murderous assault but was killed a few days later in an air crash. Philby was posted to the school from the London Headquarters and evidently hated it, not least because it cramped his activities for the Russians.

Among the staff at Brickendonbury was a man whom Philby describes as 'jolly George Hill', who was to be posted with Philby to a new school that SOE was to set up at Beaulieu.

While Philby and Hill were still at Brickendonbury with their saboteurs, Colin Gubbins was attending to the problem of setting up a training school for teaching student-agents the clandestine trade crafts. He had made a visit to Brickendonbury to study its curriculum and had added a few ideas of his own. In the late autumn of 1940 he appointed 'Jimmy' Munn as Commandant of the new school and in the early months of 1941 Munn visited the Intelligence Training Centre at Matlock in Derbyshire to start recruiting officers for the training department of the proposed new school at Beaulieu.

Chapter II

THE REQUISITIONING

According to official sources, steps were taken at the end of 1940 by SOE's London headquarters to set up a Finishing School for its secret agents, and at an early date it had been decided that the curriculum would be based on that of the MI Wing at Arisaig and the clandestine training school at Brickendonbury.

It is tempting to assume that the School was created from scratch soon after the appointment of Lieutenant-Colonel J.W.Munn early in January, 1941. But evidence from Lord Montagu's archives and several different sources, including Kim Philby, who was one of the first on the scene, indicates that prior to the founding of the Finishing School and probably prior to Gubbins' appointment as Head of Training and Operations, at least four different sections within SOE had separately made haphazard contingency plans for clandestine operations and had earmarked personnel and requisitioned premises for their training. The evidence indicates that some of the former Section D personnel at Brickendonbury were transferred to Beaulieu prior to Munn's arrival to set up a small spy school with a capacity for a handful of students. Three other sections had requisitioned houses for use as holding stations for foreign special service troops who were being held in reserve for secret operations. One of these, containing Free French parachutists, was located at Inchmery at the mouth of the Beaulieu River. It was destined to provide some of the very first SOE agents to be parachuted into occupied France, some time before the formation of the RF Section, long before any students were available from the Finishing School, and many months before the major reorganization of SOE's administration in the autumn of 1941.

In the autumn of 1940 Colin Gubbins was already busy recruiting staff for the new school. Kim Philby relates that he was summoned to attend an interview at the London headquarters and found that the atmosphere in Gubbins' office crackled with energy, so much so that Philby sat up and took notice. In a friendly tone Gubbins asked Philby, briefly, if he knew anything about political propaganda, and, when Philby said that he did,

Gubbins explained that a new training establishment was being planned 'on an ambitious scale'. Underground propoganda was to be one of the subjects in the curriculum and a suitable instructor was being sought. He invited Philby to produce a draft syllabus.

Gubbins already possessed some ideas about the organization of the school. Ideally, it needed a number of houses sited within a convenient distance of a main headquarters so that small parties of student-agents could be segregated by nationality and for security purposes to receive instruction from a central pool of peripatetic specialist instructors.

In the event it took many months to find a suitable collection of houses. The selection of Beaulieu as a suitable site for the Finishing School came about, like many of SOE's acquisitions, by the 'old boy' network. Brigadier Gerald Buckland of the 8th Ghurkas, who lived in Beaulieu and had already been recruited into SOE was aware that several houses on Lord Montagu's estate had been vacated by their owners early in the war. He suggested to Colin Gubbins that they might make excellent secret training establishments, since they were well hidden among the trees amidst the New Forest and could be easily guarded.

The existence of private country residences on the ancient Manor of Beaulieu is said to have arisen in 1905 when the second Baron Montagu suggested to a number of his friends that they might like to buy several parcels of land on his Beaulieu estate on ninety-nine year leases and build themselves substantial country houses. Most of the residences that were built lie within extensive private grounds, are out of sight of each other and out of sight of the Montagu's family seat, Palace House, and can only be approached by rough tracks or private roadways. They vary in size, some having a modest seven bedrooms, some thirteen and some nearer twenty, plus the appropriate number of reception rooms and bathrooms.

A prevalent post-war rumour insists that the SOE spy school and headquarters was established in the Montagu family home, Palace House, but in fact it was never requisitioned during the war. However, it was used as a local Air Raid Precautions headquarters and as D-Day approached it was earmarked as a stand-by headquarters for the Allied Supreme Commander, General Eisenhower.

The truth is that the first houses to be requisitioned for use for the training of secret agents were acquired piecemeal and the house which later became the headquarters of the SOE complex at Beaulieu was The Rings, which was demolished soon after the war because it was in a dilapidated state. It was situated in a wood about a mile and a half to the north-east of the present National Motor Museum, on the northern fringe of Hartford Heath close to Beaulieu Heath. It had thirteen bedrooms, three bathrooms, two reception rooms, a study and a kitchen. It was originally built in 1910 by Mr Justice Ridley, but by the outbreak of the Second World War the lease had passed to a heart specialist, Sir John Parkinson, who spent most of his time in his main residence in Devonshire Place in London.

Documents in Lord Montagu's archives reveal that SOE was not in fact the first military unit to occupy The Rings. It was first requisitioned on 21 July, 1940, to house the officers of the 9th Battalion of the King's Own Royal Regiment. Among the archives are the requisitioning order and neat hand-written lists of the furniture required to furnish it for two majors, by name Bernays and Jowers, five captains, Bentley, Castle, Dickinson, Hall and Key, and one lieutenant, Dobbyn. Each required a bed, mattress, chair and a mirror; the Commanding Officer (unnamed) and the majors were also allowed a table and an extra chair. The furnishings in the reception rooms and the hall and kitchen seem to have been requisitioned from Sir John Parkinson.

Soon after the requisitioning, Captain Widnell was harrying the authorities for compensation for the gas oil and the log wood that the Battalion had taken over with the house and for the increase in fire insurance being levied by the insurance company for requisitioned properties.

On 19 October, 1940, four months after the original requisitioning, Captain H.S.R. Widnell, the Montagu Estate's land agent, and a veteran of the First World War, received a letter from the requisitioning authorities in Southampton stating, 'It has been decided to surrender The Rings as no use can be made of it during the winter'. A month later the Battalion moved out, to Boscombe.

However, they had scarcely departed when Widnell received another letter saying that immediate arrangements had been made to reoccupy part of The Rings for a Bomb Disposal Unit, and in the same breath it stated, 'But the Section has not arrived and it is doubtful if they ever will.'

Just over a month after that, very early in January, 1941, The Rings was among the first group of properties to be requisitioned for SOE. The other properties taken over at about the same time were Hartford House, a cottage situated nearby, requisitioned at the request of its owner, The Vineyards and Boarmans, which lie half a mile to the east of Palace House and a mile to the south of The Rings. Also requisitioned at this time were two houses on the west side of the Beaulieu river. The House on the Shore and The Drokes. The Rothschild residence, Inchmery House, at

19

Inchmery on the eastern side of the Beaulieu river overlooking the Solent, four miles to the south-east of Palace House, was also requisitioned by SOE at about the same time.

Hartford House (also known as The Fisheries) was the smallest of all the houses requisitioned. Described by one of the SOE senior instructors as 'a pretty little house', it was the first of the houses to be used for segregating students from the staff by the spy school that preceded the founding of the Finishing School. After the founding it was very often unoccupied but when in use accommodated between one and three students and an instructor. It was built at the turn of the century and was part of the trout hatcheries at Hartford. At the outbreak of war it was occupied by a widower, Major Dixon.

The Vineyards and Boarmans lie to the west of the B 3054 road which runs from Hilltop and the Royal Oak pub on the edge of Beaulieu Heath down a hill into Beaulieu. The Vineyards lies on the side of a hill in an area of Palace House grounds now frequently used for special events and car rallies, and can be seen from the road just before entering Beaulieu. It was built in 1908 by Sir James Kingston Fowler, a physician to Queen Victoria and honorary warden of Beaulieu Abbey. When war was declared it was occupied by a widow, Mrs Grinnell, who left for the USA. Boarmans, which was to become famous as the preferred house for the French Section trainees, and where many women agents were trained, is not visible from the road and can only be approached by crossing a cattle grid and driving down a long private track. The house was built about 1935 by Commander E.C. Wrey who was called up at the outbreak of the war.

On the opposite side of the Beaulieu river The House on the Shore, as its name implies, is situated close to the shore of the Solent, near Sowley. It is the most isolated of all the houses requisitioned for SOE and was built for the Montagu family as a beach home in 1914 using materials from the Beaulieu estate. At the outbreak of war it was in the hands of the present Lord Montagu's mother, the Hon. Mrs Pleydell-Bouverie and had been let to Major and Mrs W.S. Wilkinson. The Drokes, which is near the west bank of the Beaulieu river, can just be seen among the trees from a boat sailing down the last reach of the river. It was built just before the First World War by Colonel Dudley Mills and at the outbreak of the Second World War was occupied by the widow of a stockbroker, Mrs Burge, who, of course, had to leave. It has thirteen bedrooms and two cottages in its 24 acres of ground. One of the cottages was occupied by her head gardener, William Durey, and his family, who were permitted to remain there throughout the SOE occupation. Thanks to William Durey's stepson, Denis Hendy, who as a boy lived in the cottage throughout the war, we have an eyewitness account of many of the events that took place at The Drokes during the early days of its occupation.

Captain Widnell usually received advanced warning of the intention of the War Office to requisition properties on the estate and advised the owners to instruct a reputable firm to take a schedule of the property.

The threat of requisitioning precipitated a barrage of paperwork between the owners' solicitors and surveyors and the requisitioning authorities in Southampton, and also between the authorities and Captain Widnell, guarding the interests of the Montagu estate. The properties had to be surveyed by the owners' representatives and later, jointly, by the authorities and a representative of the Montagu estate. Agreement had to be reached on such details as the value of the property at the time of its requisitioning, the rental to be paid by the military authorities and who would attend to and pay for the upkeep of the grounds and fences and any sheds, outhouses and cottages within the grounds. The rents payed by the Ministry of Works seem laughably small by today's standards, and were no doubt pitifully low at the time. The Rings was rented for a mere £225 per annum!

There were disputes over what rights would be accorded to the military once they had taken over. For instance, would they be allowed the use of existing garden tools, and would the existing staff, especially gardeners, continue to be employed? Some of the gardeners had been in the employ of the house-owners on the Beaulieu estate all their working lives. One appears to have lost his job after forty-two years' service.

The flurry of paperwork created by the requisitioning must have been costly and it seems that the costs had to be borne by the unfortunate owners, struggling to protect their rights and interests in their absence. Some of them were abroad on war service. No wonder that in most cases the military take-over was most unwelcome and caused considerable distress. As one of the leaseholders wrote, 'It is a bitter blow as I kept hoping (to be able to) return (to Beaulieu), though it was always postponed for one reason or another. I should be very grateful for any information as to what purpose they will use my house, if it is the same department which has taken over the other houses in Beaulieu.'

Once the requisitioning had been completed, the houses, as already stated, seem to have been allocated to several different sections within SOE during a period preceding the founding of the school, and were apparently operated independently of each other. We know that The

Rings and Hartford House were used to train some of the first secret agents and were staffed largely by instructors drawn from Brickendonbury. Official sources state that The Rings was at first in multiple use as a training headquarters, a school, and for staff and student accommodation. Since it possessed only seventeen rooms and it is known that lectures were given in the lounge, there were probably only four or five resident instructors, two administrative staff and less than half a dozen students. Philby is said to have taken a ten-day agent training course at The Rings before taking up his appointment as the Finishing School's tutor in propaganda warfare and he mentions that soon after taking up his post he was teaching black propaganda to two French trainee agents. He also mentions that a couple of Dutchmen were being trained as radio operators. He states that at this time one of the instructors was George Hill, who had moved with him from Brickendonbury.

One of the earliest students, Hardy Amies, (Sir Hardy Amies the couturier) mentioned that when he arrived the instructor in codes and cyphers was a civilian expert, thought to have been Professor Eric Patterson, also from Brickendonbury. Another source intimates that Malcolm Muggeridge was among the earliest instructors. Several of the Intelligence Corps officers who arrived later as instructors refer to Philby, Hill and Patterson as being already there.

The Drokes and The House on the Shore were first used to accommodate Spanish troops, under the command of Major J.H.P. Barcroft. Denis Hendy described him as 'a very important man' who spent much of his time in London, which suggests that he was reporting to London and not to The Rings. At a guess he belonged to the forerunner of the Iberian Section. He was assisted by Captain Barry, the 'housemaster' at The Drokes, and by Captain Tidmarsh who was 'housemaster' of The House on the Shore.

Inchmery House was taken over by Free French parachutists under Gubbins' direct intervention, and there is some evidence that The Vineyards and Boarmans were also occupied by foreign troops, possibly Italians! Lord Montagu's mother, the Hon. Mrs Pleydell-Bouverie, told me, shortly before she died, that The Vineyards was known to her as 'The Pub', because it had a drinks licence and was occasionally used by the SOE staff to entertain their civilian guests between intakes of trainees.

There seems, therefore, little doubt that in the first quarter of 1941 the training taking place in these houses was being run separately by four different sections of SOE and the courses then being run at The Rings were being run separately from the other three sections by instructors who had come from Brickendonbury, itself originally staffed by trainers from Section D of the SIS.

Denis Hendy is adamant that the first students at The Drokes were Spaniards, a fact supported by a former corporal of Field Security who was stationed at The House on the Shore. Hendy has also given a detailed description of the arrival of the British troops to take over the house in the days before the Finishing School was officially in being.

'They arrived one winter's evening at about 9pm, in the pouring rain from Brockenhurst station,' he said. 'There were about twenty of them under Captain Barry. There was a Quartermaster Sergeant, "Tansy" Lee, of the Wiltshire Regiment, Corporal Walker and Lance Corporal Stidwell. These NCOs and the Captain lived in the main house and the privates lived in the other cottage. Among the men were two from the Army Catering Corps, Privates Morris and Purdy.'

One of the soldiers whose home was nearby at Blackfield, a village on the western edge of Southampton Water, knew the Beaulieu area well but did not realize where he was until the vehicle in which the party was travelling rumbled down the hill towards Beaulieu from the direction of Brockenhurst and made the awkward, 'backhanded' turn on to the narrow road out to Buckler's Hard. On arrival at The Drokes, he lost no time in finding someone to lend him a bicycle to pedal home to visit his wife.

This party arrived a few weeks before the first intake of students, to attend to the furnishing of the rooms with standard service bedding and furniture, collecting stores and mess traps and settling in.

Denis and the Durey family were not allowed anywhere near the front of the main house and were forbidden to have any visitors, even close relatives, despite the fact that the cottage in which they lived was a quarter of a mile away from the house. Notices were posted all round the grounds forbidding anybody to enter on pain of being shot if they did. It was not an idle threat because the students and the staff used to practice using hand guns with live ammunition in the grounds and copses of the property. The Dureys rarely saw any of the visiting instructors because they always arrived in a vehicle that drove straight past the cottages and up to the house.

A regular visitor to The Drokes during this early period was Major J.H.P. Barcroft, thought by Hendy to be the first commandant of The House on the Shore but who was in fact in charge of both The Drokes and The House on the Shore. 'Barcroft,' said Hendy, 'very often came down and asked my father if he could go fishing across the marshes towards Gin's farm or off Gin's pier. He used to make regular visits to the War Office in London.' He was responsible for getting Hendy's stepfather, William Durey, who was about thirty years of age and therefore eligible for call-up, exempt from war service in the armed forces. 'He said my father was doing a far better job here feeding the troops than he would be doing if he was in the Army peeling potatoes. Mark you, my father had to cultivate three acres of land but sometimes the troops would go out and give him a hand. During the winter months I would go out with him and some of the lads, the Quartermaster Sergeant and one or other of the Corporals, into the woods and pop one or two pheasants off their roosts. We'd come back and pluck and draw them and my mother would roast them. Around 10pm about a dozen soldiers, including some of the students, would come over to our cottage for a meal of roast pheasant and fresh vegetables from the garden. My mother considered it her contribution to the war effort.'

The students seem to have mixed freely with the Durey family. Some of them used to play football with the two boys and on their recreation night, Friday night, after they had received their pay, 'they used to invite the whole family over to the house and the beer would flow and we would have a lively evening.' Hendy also stated that the women students sometimes visited his mother and borrowed her clothes, to disguise themselves during practical exercises. On one occasion one of the male students borrowed Mrs Durey's clothes to disguise himself as a woman before going out on an exercise.

Living in The House on the Shore at this time were three Spanish-speaking NCOs from the Field Security Wing of the Intelligence Corps, Corporal C.G. Holland and Lance Corporals Dicky Warden and Bernard Ettenfield.

Lance Corporal Warden was what would have been called a 'gentleman ranker' during the 1940 era, an old Etonian later to reach the rank of major in the Intelligence Corps. His Eton education left a lasting impression on some of those whom he met.

The SOE houses in the area had no resident medical officer. If any member of the staff or any of the students was too sick or incapacitated to visit an army clinic, a local GP was sent for. This was a well-known Lymington doctor, Dr Basil Thornton, who was unfit for military service. He was a partner in a practice which in pre-war days dealt with the gentry in the Beaulieu area. On the first occasion that he was called to attend to a patient at The House on the Shore he was met outside the house by Lance Corporal Warden. Warden charmingly warned him that when he

24

stepped through the door into the house he would be entering another world and one which, afterwards, he would have to forget, and forget everything that he had seen or heard, on pain of dire but unspecified penalties.

During the war Dr Thornton visited several of the SOE houses to attend to patients and was occasionally invited to cocktail parties and social events held from time to time during change-over periods between student intakes at The Vineyards and The House in the Wood, which was soon to be requisitioned for use as the officers' mess.

There is clearly no doubt that before the Finishing School officially came into existence, piecemeal training was already taking place at Beaulieu. Munn's arrival marked the integration of these fragmented arrangements and the absorption of The Rings teaching team of Philby, George Hill and Professor E.J. Patterson into the team of instructors brought down from the Intelligence Corps depot at Matlock.

Within three months of the requisitioning of The Rings it had become too small to accommodate the school's administration as well as housing the administrative and teaching staff and students. A house near The Rings called The House in the Woods, which had been one of three of Lord Montagu's four residences on the Beaulieu estate, was requisitioned for use as an officers' mess for the administrative and teaching staff of the school. And the students were moved out of The Rings and into the other houses in the complex.

The House in the Woods had been built in about 1910 and contained over thirty rooms. At the time of its requisitioning it belonged to Vivian Drury who had gone to the Bahamas as First Equerry to the Duke of Windsor. It is the only one of the houses used by SOE that is still remembered locally, and incorrectly, as a house where spies were trained during the Second World War.

Almost a year later more student accommodation became necessary and early in 1942 the piecemeal requisitioning began of four more houses on the Montagu estate. Saltmarsh was acquired on 6 January, Warren House, on to the west of the Beaulieu river overlooking the Solent near Needs Oar Point, was taken over on 6 March; Blackbridge, adjacent to Saltmarsh was requisitioned on 7 June and finally, Clobb Gorse, also to the west of the Beaulieu River, close to Buckler's Hard, was acquired in October, 1942.

Saltmarsh is the only one of these houses visible to the public; it is situated on the outskirts of Beaulieu, by the road to Lyndhurst. It was built in 1931 by Captain G. Rockingham Gill, a yacht designer who was called up at the outbreak of the war. Blackbridge was the home of Lady Austen Chamberlain, but it had been rented to the Hon. Mrs Murray. Its furniture had been put into store before it was requisitioned for the sum of £260 p.a.

Warren House is near The House on the Shore and was originally known as Warren Farm House. It had been substantially renovated in the 1920s and 30s and had been let to a businessman, Mr C.R. Coomber, a year before war was declared. It was to become a school for training agents in the use of carrier pigeons and micro-photography. Clobb Gorse, which is near The Drokes, was built in 1927 and at the time it was requisitioned was occupied by Mr and Mrs J. Wilby.

These acquisitions provided the new school with nine houses for student accommodation and were sufficiently dispersed to keep students of different nationalities segregated for security purposes, so that if any of them had the misfortune to be caught on operations they could not identify agents of other Occupied countries.

In theory the new school's capacity was now eighty students undergoing training simultaneously. However, official records state that this number was never reached. One reason was that for tuition purposes the students had to be segregated not just by nationality but also according to the type and length of training they were receiving. They were being trained for at least five different types of secret service.

Inchmery House, the Rothschild property situated at the mouth of the Beaulieu river overlooking the Solent, requisitioned at about the same time as The Rings, was originally occupied by twenty-five Free French parachutists, who had recently obtained their 'wings' from the British parachutist school at Ringway near Manchester. They were soon to be placed under the control of the BCRA. Although Inchmery House was part of the Beaulieu SOE complex and drew some of its instructors from the Finishing School, it was not regarded as an integral part of the Beaulieu school. It was later to be used by the Polish secret services and by British commandos working for SOE and has a particularly interesting wartime history.

Chapter III

THE FINISHING SCHOOL

The Finishing School actually evolved over a period of twenty-two months, between January, 1941, and October, 1942, but by the spring of 1941 it had taken a form that was familiar to the thousands of people who trained there.

By April, 1941, each of the houses in the complex was being officially described as a Group B Special Training School (STS). The Rings became STS 31, Hartford House STS 32 (but later renumbered 31, part of the HQ), The House on the Shore STS 33, the Drokes STS 34, The Vineyards STS 35 and Boarmans STS 36. In March, 1941, The House in the Wood was requisitioned as the officers' mess for the school staff and became part of STS 31. The later acquisitions which occurred between January and October, 1942, long after Munn's departure, were grouped in pairs to form two additional 'schools'. Saltmarsh and nearby Blackbridge to the north of the tidal part of the Beaulieu River became STS 32a and b respectively, a single administrative unit. Warren House and Clobb Gorse, west of the Beaulieu River, became STS 37a and b, again a single administrative unit. Inchmery House became STS 38.

The first Commandant of the new school, Lieutenant-Colonel J.W. Munn, had started his career with SOE teaching map-reading and fieldcraft at the commando school at Arisaig, and was subsequently promoted and put in command of it. Philby described him as a young colonel of the sensible military type and added that at Beaulieu 'Jimmy' Munn had 'held together a school of pretty odd fish in a net of personal authority'. Munn stayed at Beaulieu for only six months, barely enough time to set up the school and get it running before he was posted to Canada to set up a similar school there. Later he was sent to Algeria, at that time a French colony, to take charge of the SOE operational base called Massingham on the coast of North Africa near Algiers. But he was essentially an administrator and had no previous experience of teaching spy crafts or of running operations. He is said to have come unstuck at Massingham, unable to cope with the task or with the diplomacy required to deal with the political cross-currents and rivalries of various French political factions. He was eventually transferred to the Secret Intelligence Service to take up a senior training post.

He arrived in Beaulieu in January with a small staff which at first lived and worked in The Rings. Among the new arrivals was the school's first Adjutant, the rotund and balding Captain (soon to be promoted to Major) Palmer, a veteran of the First World War. He did the donkey work in organizing the school and was helped by Captain Parsons, the Administrative Officer. Also among the first batch of officers were four or five to act as adjutants, that is, 'housemasters', of the student houses, among them Captain R. Carr, who remained at Beaulieu for the rest of the war.

The size of the staff needed to man the schools in the Beaulieu complex had been determined by an Army manning schedule, called a War Establishment. It specified the number of cooks, batmen, clerks and drivers, NCOs and officers considered necessary to meet the predicted needs of each school. Many of the men detailed to staff the houses had already settled into them by the time Munn and his team arrived and they had been drawn from all sorts of regiments and corps. The original War Establishment, later adjusted, 'allowed, in addition to the permanent staff, a lieutenant-colonel in command, a major administrative officer and second-in-command, a major chief instructor, a major assistant chief instructor, eight captain instructors and six subaltern instructors,' a total of eighteen officers plus a captain-adjutant for each of the four main student houses. As the war progressed it was found impossible to find officers of the rank of subaltern with sufficient qualifications to act as instructors and they had to be replaced with officers of the rank of captain, giving an establishment of twenty-two captains in all. It was later increased to twenty-six.

There was a continuous turnover of both officers and men throughout the war. The fitter regimental officers and men of the administrative staff were soon replaced by older men and the physically less fit and as the instructors gained experience they were sent abroad to set up similar schools. However, several of the original administrative and teaching staff remained at Beaulieu for the rest of the war.

STS 31, comprising The Rings, The House in the Wood and Hartford House, had a total staff of about seventy. It had three senior NCOs, including a Physical Training Instructor, eight batmen, five mess orderlies, four cooks, only three clerks, twelve vehicle drivers, including a mechanic, a storeman and seven general dutymen. It was allowed one 15 cwt truck, two cars, two pick-ups and one motor cycle.

The staffs of the houses allocated as student residences varied slightly in size according to the size of the house or houses, but the basic staff allowance for each 'school' was one sergeant-major or sergeant, one corporal, one clerk, two orderlies, two cooks, three or four batmen, one driver to drive the pick-up vehicle with which each school was provided and one motor cycle orderly to drive each school's motor cycle. There were also a fair number of Field Security personnel sprinkled among the houses acting as instructors or interpreters and they had the additional burden of having to perform their main FS duties in the Beaulieu area, visiting local pubs to check on careless talk among all the service customers, to look out for, and listen to members of the SOE staff, and watch for students straying out of bounds of their houses.

It is estimated that the total complement of the Beaulieu Finishing School, excluding the staff of Inchmery House, and not counting a continuous stream of visiting instructors and conducting officers, was thirty officers, fifteen sergeants and about 130 junior NCOs and Other Ranks, a total complement of 175.

The identities of the first batch of NCOs and Other Ranks to man The Rings before Munn's arrival is not known, but later arrivals included Sergeant Fielding, Corporal Don Butchers, the head driver, and Private Jock Flockhart who became the Commandant's driver and drove a large American sedan car, a Hudson Terraplane. Don Butchers had been a steeplechase jockey and after the war returned to horse racing and eventually became a trainer.

The Rings had to provide office accommodation for about thirty-three people. The forty or so junior Other Ranks were dispatched to arrange their sleeping quarters in the cottages and outhouses within the grounds. Some time later barrack huts were built within the grounds for the ORs and the cottages were used for other purposes. It is believed that the senior NCOs lived in the main house. Office accommodation was allocated according to rank.

In the spring two civilian secretaries arrived from SOE's London headquarters, Miss Dorothy Wickens, affectionately known as 'Wicky', the Commandant's secretary, and Mrs Phil Spridell, whose husband was a corporal serving in North Africa. She was later replaced by Evadne Cull. They were housed in one of the cottages within the grounds of The Rings from which the soldiers had been evicted, and were well looked after by a civilian housekeeper, Miss Richardson, known to the secretaries as Rickie.

In August they were joined by a third secretary, Ann Keenlyside, who has provided a substantial amount of information on the organization of the school and the identities and roles of members of the staff. She had been recruited into SOE through a secretarial agency, which had offered her jobs with a gynaecologist, the Political Warfare Executive or the Inter-Services Research Bureau - the cover name for SOE. She chose the latter and was sent for an interview at Baker Street. On appointment she was immediately posted to Beaulieu.

The three secretaries were the only women on the school's administrative staff. In many of the other SOE establishments the female staff – domestic, secretarial and drivers – was provided by the First Aid Nursing Yeomanry, the FANYs, but there were never any of them at Beaulieu where the domestic and clerical chores and all the driving was done by soldiers throughout the School's existence. Later in the war two Officers of the FANY joined the teaching staff.

The Rings became a functional headquarters. On the ground floor was the Commandant's office, the Adjutant's office and a room accommodating his three clerks. Also on the ground floor was the NCOs' mess and the original kitchens. The Other Ranks are also thought to have had their mess on the ground floor, although their sleeping quarters were elsewhere.

On the first floor there was an office accommodating the three secretaries but was otherwise entirely occupied by the training staff, including storerooms for their supplies, epidiascopes and articles used for demonstration purposes, such as wall charts and a collection of German uniforms. The two senior instructors shared a room and the rest were packed into the remaining bedrooms, three or four to a room.

In March The House in the Wood, which has over thirty rooms, had been taken over as an officers' mess for members of the staff. The reception rooms are not large and must have been somewhat crowded when occupied by all the officers simultaneously. The House in the Wood is indeed buried in a wood and can only be approached by driving up a long track through woodland which, beyond the house, ultimately leads to an area known as Hartford Heath and a large gravel roundabout surrounding a small island of tall trees. Other tracks lead, in one direction, from the roundabout through the woods to The Rings and Hartford House and in another across Great Goswell Copse to The Vineyards and Boarmans. There are also tracks within the woods that lead westwards to Saltmarsh and Blackbridge, two more student houses. To the south is Palace House, the home of the Montagus. These houses are within walking distance of each other, although it is a fairly long walk, but it was often made in the dead of night by small groups of trainee agents sneaking along the gravel tracks trying not to make a noise when out on burglary and housebreaking exercises.

The administration and training departments were functionally separate but shared some of the administrative duties and some of the domestic and training supervision of the students. The Adjutant, Major Palmer, (later replaced by Major Alan Wilkinson) headed the administration, and Major S.H.C. Woolrych, whom we have yet to meet, was the Chief Instructor until promoted to the role of Commandant of the school in April when Munn moved on.

The administration was responsible for the running of the nine student accommodation houses. The 'housemasters' were veterans of the First World War, 'Funny old dug-ups,' as one of the younger instructors described them, and came from a variety of regiments, were fluent in a foreign language, usually French, and were about twenty years older than the instructors.

The main administration at The Rings negotiated with the various SOE Country Sections in London for places at the school, attended to the allocation of students to the various houses and had the custody of their personal files. The Commandant had the responsibility for completing a report on the performance of all students, for submission to the head of whichever Country Section had sponsored them. It was the Country Section which made the decision on whether or not the student would be dispatched as a secret agent, and there are many well-publicized instances where women students were sent on active service despite adverse reports from the school. Some of them lost their lives in dreadful circumstances.

The dispersal of both the domestic and teaching arrangements among the nine student residences was not without its problems. The need to conceal from the students the existence and location of the other student houses, and the segregation of the students by nationality and often by their future functions, required an organization of some complexity and was a nightmare for those responsible for timetabling the syllabus.

The secrecy surrounding the whole enterprise was such that the students undergoing training at the various houses never knew the names of the houses in which they resided, unless they happened to know the area from pre-war experience, which very few of them did. Secrecy also gave rise to a number of rumours among the students about the administration of the school and its location. They were deliberately kept in ignorance of the central day-to-day administration, or took it for granted, and therefore make no reference to it in their personal reminiscences. They usually knew where it was located because The Rings was the target of many of the housebreaking and burglary exercises, but many of them believed that the name of the house was 'Beaulieu Manor', which is in fact the name of the entire Montagu estate. Almost every student who subsequently wrote about his or her experiences at Beaulieu stated that the school's headquarters was housed in 'Beaulieu Manor, the home of Lord Montagu'! Even M.R.D. Foot, in one of his histories, states that the school's headquarters was located in 'Beaulieu Manor, on the site where the National Motor Museum now stands'. In fact the Motor Museum is sited in the parkland near Palace House.

Many of the personal reminiscences of the trainees make a point of explaining that students of particular nationalities were always allocated to particular houses. For instance it has been repeatedly stated that the Norwegian and Dutch students were always put into houses overlooking the Solent to make them feel more at home with the presence of water. But this is a rumour since it is known for certain that Dutch students were also accommodated in Hartford House, adjacent to The Rings and Saltmarsh, which is above the millpond at the very top of the Beaulieu River. The Norwegians are known to have been accommodated in almost all of the student houses at various times during the war. There is, however, some substance in the rumour that the French Section had a preference for, but not exclusive use of, Boarmans for their students, among them the very first batch of women trainee agents.

The management of the entire school staff, officers and other ranks, the allocation of duties, leave rotas, the issuing of pay to staff and students, catering, the drawing and issuing of supplies, and disciplinary matters were all duties of the administration.

The functions of the houses in the SOE complex varied during the course of the war and was complicated by the constantly changing policy regarding the security training of student radio operators of all the Country Sections and by the handing over to the Free French BCRA of Inchmery House, initially for the training of their radio-operators. Most of the Country Sections seem to have preferred to keep the W/T operators separate from other kinds of trainee agents, such as couriers, organizers or saboteurs. The reason was that radio operators were very vulnerable to detection and a high percentage of them were caught by the Nazis.

The security training of radio operators seems to have provided the school with a continuous administrative headache. They were often young and irresponsible and were considered by higher authorities to be 'a considerable danger to the organization in the field', a fact underlined by the appalling losses of those trained for the RF Section at Inchmery House. At first those undergoing W/T training for the other Country Sections were given only rudimentary training in security while learning their telegraphy skills and procedures, but this was evidently unsatisfactory and they were sent on a course which was a mixture of W/T and security training. In the spring of 1942 it was changed again and became a ten-day security course. It was changed yet again to a full two-week security course at Beaulieu, during which they had to continue with daily W/T practice.

The Commandant and his Adjutant, Captain Palmer, had to keep the peace between military personnel and the civilian population and liaise with Captain Widnell and the Beaulieu estate office on a wide variety of matters concerning trespass of their troops, drunken pranks with 'borrowed' property like bicycles, motor cycles and in one instance a horse, major and minor damage to property, the punishment of offenders and the interpretation of military and civil rights.

On 5 June, 1941, Captain Widnell wrote to Munn pointing out in no uncertain terms that civilians walking legitimately on the Beaulieu estate had been stopped by Captain Parsons and told they would be prosecuted. Widnell pointed out that SOE had requisitioned only certain isolated properties and that 'access to other houses, rides, woods etc have not been the subject of any communication regarding requisitioning.' He continued, 'I shall be only too happy to go into the whole question fully with you to ascertain exactly what it is that you require in the way of extra privacy.' He concluded, 'If these regulations interfere with the usual enjoyment and use of any portion of the estate, the matter must be put through the usual channels and I shall naturally be obliged to claim compensation.'

It was a sharp reminder that SOE had not requisitioned the entire Montagu estate, only small bits of it, and had no right to interfere with country life outside the grounds of the houses that they had requisitioned. Throughout the war Captain Widnell kept up a lively barrage of communication with the school's successive Commandants over a variety of matters concerning the Army's rights and the damage caused to woodlands by the depredations of military exercises and vehicles crashing into hedges. In one of these exercises 150 saplings of sycamore, ash, birch and alder were cut down without permission in furtherance of some field exercise.

After the fall of France in May, 1940, until 22 June, 1941, when the Nazis invaded Russia, Britain was continuously under the threat of a German invasion. Beaulieu was in a very vulnerable area and within a coastal defence belt. From the outset the staff of all the houses, like every other service unit in the area, were involved in preparations for the defence of the coast and had to take an active part in defence plans. They had to undergo regular weapons and explosives training in disused quarries. One of the houses, The House on the Shore, is right on the coast at the head of a beach and seems to have been earmarked as a defensive point from which members of the School staff were required to repel any attempted landing.

In Lord Montagu's archives is a collection of photographs of labels on cupboard doors in The House on the Shore which read 'Boxes of Grenades not to be primed until Action Stations is given.' and 'Boxes of .32 (ammunition) not to be opened until Action Stations is given'.

Part of the SOE plan for the defence of the area was to organize 'stay behind' parties drawn from members of the School staff to carry out guerrilla warfare once the area was overrun by the enemy. For this purpose a very well known member of the School staff, Captain William Clark, a highly skilled woodsman and former gamekeeper from the royal estate at Sandringham, had secretly constructed hideouts, one of which was a large hole in the floor of the New Forest, somewhere in the Beaulieu area. It was superbly hidden and indistinguishable from its surroundings in the forest and could not be detected even by somebody walking over it. It was large enough to house the stay-behind party and all their food, weapons and ammunition. The idea was that the party would emerge at night and attach limpet mines with delayed fuses to the tracks of German tanks and vehicles. It was used during several defence exercises, before the threat of invasion had faded after the German invasion of Russia.

Chapter IV

STATION 36

The Crucible of Action

Inchmery House was known to the British as STS (Special Training School) 38, to the French as Station 36, or, more affectionately, as '*La Pouce Marie*', and was probably known by the Poles by some other number.

The house was originally the home of the Rothschild family, before they moved into Exbury House, and it was requisitioned by SOE in the spring of 1941, at about the same time that the first batch of houses had been requisitioned on the Montagu estate at Beaulieu.

During much of the war it was used to house various small specialist groups of commandos that were part of the SOE organization. In the middle of the war the house was taken over for some months by the Polish 6th Bureau (Secret Service) and afterwards reverted to use by SOE.

Official records are vague on the issue of whether it was originally intended to be an integral part of the Beaulieu Finishing School. In the official history of the SOE in France, Inchmery House is classified as the RF Section's preliminary commando training school on a par with F Section's school at Wanborough Manor near Guildford, but it was plunged into training Free French saboteurs a month or so before the main school came into use and many of these men were parachuted into France some months before the Beaulieu-trained agents were sent on active service. Throughout its wartime history it remained an unwanted and unloved appendage to the main SOE complex at Beaulieu.

Yet Inchmery House can claim to have played a very significant part in the history of SOE, not just because it produced some of the first agents to be parachuted into France, but because their success led to the strengthening of SOE's position in its early struggles for its own survival.

In 1940 France had fallen to the Nazis and had been split into two zones. The northern part had been occupied by German forces and the southern part, known as the Unoccupied Zone, was governed on their behalf by the French Government at Vichy. Britain was threatened with a German invasion, SOE was in its infancy and the Country Sections were still in the process of being set up. Few, if any secret agents had yet been trained by the British or by any of the Governments-in-exile.

At the end of 1940, at the height of the German's nightly bombardment of British cities, known as 'the blitz', somebody in our own Air Ministry asked SOE if it could mount an operation to kill the German 'pathfinder' pilots of the Kampfgeschwader 100 at an air base in Meucon in Brittany. The task of these pilots was to lead the German bombers to their targets, using radio beams to fix their position, and our scientists were experiencing a great deal of trouble devising countermeasures to jam or bend the beams. On 6 November, 1940, one of these specially equipped German aircraft had run out of fuel and had landed by mistake, intact, on a beach at Bridport in Dorset! Somebody in Air Intelligence had discovered, probably by interrogating the crew of this aircraft or from questioning German bomber crews who had been shot down over this country, that the pathfinder pilots were being ferried from their quarters to the airfield in buses, thereby providing an opportunity to kill them all in one blow and severely disrupt the nightly devastation of our cities.

At this point the then head of SOE, Sir Frank Nelson, had not yet received his first operational directive from the British Chiefs of Staff, although a few tentative clandestine operations were being made to put a handful of agents into France by sea and air, and recover them.

The Free French Section of SOE, i.e. the RF Section, had not yet come into being and General de Gaulle and his staff were being deliberately kept in the dark about SOE's earliest attempts to land and recover agents.

The French Section of SOE (as distinct from the Free French RF Section) had no trained agents available and so Colin Gubbins, who currently held the post of Director of Training and Operations, and his deputy R.H. Barry, took over the organization of the mooted operation. They approached General de Gaulle and his Chief Intelligence Officer, Andre Dewavrin (Colonel Passy) to ask their permission to borrow some Free French troops then undergoing training as parachutists at the British parachutist's training school at Ringway airport, near Manchester. Apparently they did not reveal why they were required but nonetheless were given permission to use these men. However, Gubbins and Barry did not have the means of delivering them to France.

Even though it had been the Air Ministry that had asked for the operation, when it came to the point of having to assign aircraft to the task the Chief of the Air Staff, Sir Charles Portal, and the head of Bomber

Command, Sir Arthur ('Bomber') Harris tried to insist that the parachutists should be dressed in their uniforms and should not be dropped in civilian clothes. To quote from M.R.D. Foot's official history, *S.O.E. in France*, Sir Charles Portal remarked, 'I think that the dropping of men dressed in civilian clothes for the purpose of killing members of the opposing forces is not an operation with which the Royal Air Force should be associated.'

This was typical of the attitude of the Establishment regarding the conduct of war and characterized the distaste that many senior commanders and ministers retained throughout the war for SOE's 'dirty and underhanded' methods. They had no objection to soldiers being dropped in uniform to murder the enemy! Gubbins had much difficulty in getting the Air Ministry to provide a bomber to convey the parachutists to France.

Another last-minute complication erupted when de Gaulle discovered that the British had been sending agents into France behind his back. He decreed that henceforth none of his men were to take part in any operation unless he was given full details.

By this time two groups of Free French soldiers, about fifty of them, had already qualified as parachutists at Ringway and were waiting in a camp at Camberley. Many of these men were very young and the manner by which they had come to this country is interesting. When France fell to the Germans in the early summer of 1940 a number of influential Frenchmen had organized the evacuation to England of over 800 French youths of 17 and 18 years of age. They arrived in Britain in the Belgian ship *Prince Leopold*, later requisitioned by the Royal Navy and converted to an Infantry Landing Ship. They were accommodated in the exhibition centre at Olympia in London where they were later addressed by General de Gaulle on a recruiting mission for the Free French Forces. Some of these young men volunteered for special duties and were inducted into the Free French army for basic army training. They were then sent in batches for parachute training at Ringway. Many of them were formed into a unit which was to develop into a regiment similar to our own Special Air Service and others were drafted into a unit known as the Chasseur Battalion.

Among the officers of the unit which was to become the 1st Air Infantry Company, was a 30-year-old French regular soldier, Captain Georges Berge. On 20 December, 1940, he was interviewed by Commandant d'Estienne d'Orves, the chief of the French Deuxième Bureau (Secret Service). Berge drew his attention to the advantages of parachuting into France on moonlit nights. The Commandant responded by saying that it was an interesting proposition but before it could be contemplated the parachutists ought to undertake a course of special training to equip them for duties as secret agents.

As a result of this interview Berge and ten of his men were sent in February, 1941, to STS 17, the British Secret Service's sabotage and assassination training school at Brickendonbury. While at this school Berge was approached by a representative of the Deuxième Bureau accompanied by an unknown British officer and was invited to carry out an important mission in Brittany.

Eight days later Berge, accompanied by Colin Gubbins and two other officers, sought approval for the mission from the prickly General de Gaulle, who gave his approval for what became known as Operation Savanna.

Captain Berge and four of his men, in civilian clothes, were parachuted into France on the night of 14 March, 1941. Their mission was to kill the busload of German pathfinder pilots of the Kampfgeschwader 100 with a specially made road trap. Unfortunately for the raiding party, the pilots were no longer being transported by bus, but were driving to their airfield in cars with only two or three airmen in each car!

With no target to attack, Berge dispersed his team and spent his time making a reconnaissance to sound out the local population about their willingness to participate in anti-German activities on behalf of General de Gaulle and generally taking note of living conditions under the Nazis. With another member of his team, he travelled to Paris, Nevers and Bordeaux. On 23 March, during his visit, he set up a reception committee and a liaison network for future operations at Mirmizan near the Atlantic coast south of Bordeaux in a sparsely inhabited area of France known as Les Landes.

While at Nevers he took a day off to slip across into unoccupied France to visit his prospective father-in-law to formally ask him for his daughter's hand in marriage. The daughter worked in de Gaulle's headquarters in London. Returning again to the Nazi occupied zone he met up at the end of the month with two other members of his team at Sables d'Olonne on the Atlantic coast in the Bay of Biscay between St Nazaire and La Rochelle to await recovery by a British submarine. After waiting several nights for their pick-up, the submarine *HMS Tigris* appeared on the night of 4 April, but the weather was so rough that two of the three canoes which were to come ashore to collect the party were wrecked and only one made it to the shore to rescue Berge and only one other parachutist, Forman. The third, Letac, had to be left behind. The rescuing canoeist was Geoffrey

Appleyard of the Small Scale Raiding Force, a unit later to become an integral part of SOE with a troop based at Inchmery House.

Although Operation Savanna was a failure, it proved that the methods of delivery and recovery of agents were effective, and that the agents could move about inside France with relative ease. In addition to proving that operations were possible, Berge brought back with him a mass of intelligence about living conditions, curfew and many other rules, identity papers, ration cards and prices of cigarettes and essential goods and materials, and invaluable information about railway travel – intelligence that SOE had vainly sought for months.

On his return, Berge was lionized by Colonel Passy, and senior people in SOE, was awarded the British Military Cross and met the Prime Minister and his wife. Afterwards he was posted to Inchmery House to prepare his troops for another mission.

There was a small number of Free French parachutists at Inchmery at this time undergoing training as intelligence officers, saboteurs and secret wireless operators. The house itself was run by a British officer of SOE's RF Section, which had just come into being to liaise with the Free French Secret Service, then in the process of creating the BCRA.

There were about fifteen members of the administrative and instruction staff at Inchmery House at this time. The instructors were mostly French, but the principal instructor in sabotage and explosives was a British officer, Lieutenant John Seeds, the elegant son of a diplomat. The day-to-day running of the house was entrusted initially to Sergeant Chef François Baconnais who had lost an eye during the retreat from Dunkirk.

On 15 April, 1941, shortly after the return of the Savanna pair, the RF Section of SOE in conjunction with the Free French Secret Service, began planning another raid, Operation Josephine B, a proposed attack on an electric transformer station at Pessac which provided power to the German submarine base at Bordeaux. The Battle of the Atlantic was being fought against German U-boats which were threatening to strangle this country of essential war materials and food supplies, and anything that could be done to hinder the German menace would make a significant contribution to the survival of beleaguered Britain.

Berge was given the job of selecting men for the operation. He went to Inchmery House and selected a team of three – Forman, who had been on Operation Savanna, Varnier and Cabard – and set about training them at Inchmery for the new mission.

The trio were parachuted into France on the night of 11/12 May. The official report says that they were parachuted blind near Bordeaux, but

Berge (who survived the war and became a General) says that they were dropped at Mimizan near the Atlantic coast to the reception committee that he had arranged during his time in France in March on the Savanna operation.

The full story of the adventures of the Josephine B team is given in Foot's history of SOE in France. It did not go smoothly; their plans were upset by the discovery of electrified security fencing round the target area. The attack was postponed, the trio missed their submarine pick-up and fled to Paris where they made contact with Joel Letac, the man Geoffrey Appleyard had been compelled to leave on the beach because of bad weather after Savanna. The four parachutists returned to the Bordeaux area, found their target unguarded except for a night watchman and the electrified security fence, and with very considerable ingenuity got into the premises. They attached their explosive and incendiary charges to the transformers and as they were cycling away the charges exploded, destroying six out of eight transformers. The power supplies to south-west France were seriously disrupted for many months, affecting not only the supplies to the German submarine base but also to local factories producing war materials for the Germans and the electric railway system over a wide area. All four of the saboteurs eventually returned to Britain after many adventures.

The effects of Savanna and Josephine B on SOE's struggle for survival in the face of persistent attempts by other secret services and the armed forces to destroy it was considerable. It proved that a handful of trained agents could be landed and recovered successfully, could operate in enemy territory and inflict damage out of proportion to their numbers. It is ironic that SOE's future was in no small part saved not by 'conventional' Beaulieu-trained secret agents but by Free French SAS-type parachutists trained at Inchmery House! This did in fact presage developments in SOE's recruitment policy which was eventually to turn increasingly to the use of Special Forces troops instead of the commando-trained secret agents masquerading as civilians.

At the time of the attack on Pressac Inchmery House was the base for Berge and eight other officers, nineteen NCOs and seventy men, most of whom were exceedingly young. One of their number was a 19-year-old private, Gerard Brault, ultimately to be trained at Inchmery as a secret agent. Brault reported that they were undergoing a very tough commando training régime in the Southampton and Bournemouth areas.

In June they had a visit from Captain R. Lagier, one of the architects of Josephine B and a member of the SA Section of the BCRA (a section roughly equivalent to SO 2 division of SOE). Lagier selected twenty-one of the parachutists for special operations in France and as they completed their training at Inchmery they were posted to other schools for more specialized training. The rest of the Company, seventy-seven of them including Captain Georges Berge, left for the Middle East on 16 July, 1941, and were replaced in August by another, smaller group of trained French parachutists.

Berge's Free French paratroopers played a significant part in operations behind the German lines in the North African campaign and suffered exceptionally heavy casualties. Berge and another officer, Lieutenant Jordan, and about a dozen of their men joined David Stirling's SAS and eventually became its Free French Squadron. Berge did his SAS training with Fitzroy Maclean who commented in his book *Eastern Approaches* on the remarkable zeal and tenacity of the Frenchman. They received further training in explosives and sabotage from that notable SAS character Bill 'One Jump' Cumper of the Royal Engineers, reputed to know all there was to be known about demolition.

In June, 1942, David Stirling organized a series of raids on German airfields in North Africa and elsewhere, the aim of which was to disrupt and cripple the German squadrons throughout the Mediterranean area while a convoy of British warships and merchantmen was making its dash through the Mediterranean to Egypt. All of these raids were carried out by the Free French Squadron of the SAS. Commandant Georges Berge led a team of Frenchmen and one British SAS officer, the renowned George Jellicoe, on a raid on Heraklion airfield in Crete in June, 1942, during which they destroyed twenty-one enemy aircraft, four trucks and a petrol dump. Afterwards they were betrayed by a Cretan peasant and only Jellicoe escaped capture and was retrieved by a submarine. Berge and his men were last seen engaged in a pitched battle with the enemy. He survived and spent the rest of the war as a prisoner of war of the Germans.

The Free French Squadron of the SAS suffered terrible casualties during this series of raids.

The young Frenchmen who replaced the first group at Inchmery House arrived on 15 August, 1941. There were three officers, including cadet Louis Kerjean, and about ten other ranks, among them Gerard Brault, Georges Ledoux and Daniel Cordier. They were supervised by Paul Schmidt, who despite his name was French and was later parachuted into France to organize the considerable and growing clandestine traffic of French politicians and secret agents into and out of that country. Sometime during August they received a visit from General de Gaulle who watched them put on a display using explosives. It was shortly after this visit that Lieutenant Seeds lost a hand while handling a detonator. The previous day a French tutor had lost two fingers in the same way. The next day Seeds, seeking the cause of the accident and suspecting that the detonators were faulty, held one in his left hand so that if it did explode he would not lose his dominant hand. It was indeed faulty and it blew off his left hand. He was carried across the lawns of Inchmery House by his students and was rushed into Lymington hospital for treatment. He was replaced by Captain Johnson.

As the students finished their six months of training or were sent on operations they were replaced by other young Frenchmen. Some of them were taught some of their trade crafts by British instructors and lecturers borrowed from SOE and from the Finishing School at Beaulieu.

The French students were a high-spirited group and, unlike their counterparts in the Beaulieu complex, they seem to have been allowed out of the grounds of Inchmery House into the surrounding area whenever they were off duty. There are numerous stories of their pranks using small explosive charges. On one occasion they fitted a charge to some railway lines that had been laid within the grounds of the house and attached a trip wire out of the grounds and across the road from Inchmery to Lepe. An unfortunate car driver drove into it triggering off a blast. Badly shaken, the poor man took a lot of convincing that he had been the victim of a prank and not a serious attempt to kill him. On another occasion they raided the RAF base at Calshot and placed dummy charges on numerous aircraft and buildings, to the fury of the base commander. He had much cause for anger not only because of the breach of protocol but because his base was being used to man and service four Heinkel HE 115 seaplanes, formerly of the Royal Norwegian Air Force, but now painted in the full camouflage and regalia of the German Luftwaffe and belonging to a Special Duties Squadron carrying spies in their floats to many parts of northern and southern Europe for MI 6, the Secret Intelligence Service!

According to one of the senior Beaulieu instructors the discipline and sense of security of the French students and staff was appalling by British standards and the Finishing School staff avoided making any unnecessary formal contact with them. However, the staff of the two schools did mix informally. The French food at Inchmery House was far superior to that served up in the officers' mess at The House in the Woods or in any of the student houses, and the British officers looked forward to dining there occasionally and used the opportunity to brush up their French.

There were important differences and few similarities in the syllabus of the two courses. The Beaulieu students did their para-military training elsewhere, whereas the French school at Inchmery was regarded by the British, but not by the French, as primarily a para-military training base where parachutists did their commando training. Beaulieu did not specialize in training students in demolition techniques, whereas Inchmery did, using live explosives. Railway lines had been laid in the grounds to the west of Inchmery House so that the trainee saboteurs could practise laying charges. They were also taken to Brockenhurst station and goods yard to learn to drive steam engines and to rehearse laying demolition charges on real railway lines and sets of points. One of the French students, Daniel Cordier, related that small teams were 'dropped' from the back of a lorry somewhere in the New Forest and, using their maps and compasses, had to find the railway line to London and at a predetermined spot lay specimen charges in time to 'catch' a train passing at three o'clock in the morning. The teams frequently got lost; sometimes they stumbled into the bogs for which the Forest is notorious, got themselves plastered in mud and on one occasion were so seriously delayed extricating themselves that they were unable to lay their charges until after 6 am, three hours after their train had passed!

Between July and October, 1941, at least six two-man teams trained at Inchmery were infiltrated into France, usually by parachute. Each team consisted of an organizer and a radio operator, both extremely young, in their late teens or early twenties.

One of the earliest Inchmery-trained resistance organizers was Lieutenant Henri Labit who became one of the heroes of the Resistance. With his radio operator, Cartigny, he was parachuted into Normandy in the late spring of 1941 to investigate the feasibility of making a sabotage attack on a large German air base near Caen. Labit spent two days on reconnaissance, actually getting into the base by swapping places with a labourer working in the air base. Afterwards he sent a report back to London. He and his radio operator subsequently ran into difficulties with the Germans. Cartigny was arrested and was never seen again, presumably shot. Labit hid in a stream and escaped detection. He eventually made his way to Toulouse, in the unoccupied zone of France, where he set up a resistance group. He was joined in October by Warrant Officer Forman, one of the original Savanna team, on his third mission, and two radio operators. Forman had expansive plans for organizing a large resistance group, while Labit spent his time training volunteers in underground warfare in the suburbs of Toulouse.

The Vichy police caught the two radio operators. Forman and Labit fled first to Paris and then to Brittany where they joined up with another group of RF Section agents including Joel Letac, another of the original Savanna team. On the last night of the year 1941 they were all retrieved from the coast of Brittany by a British Motor Gun Boat.

Henri Labit returned to France in April, 1942, but soon afterwards he was cornered at a wayside station south of Bordeaux while trying to cross the frontier into the unoccupied zone. He tried to shoot his way out of trouble but was faced with an overwhelming number of German troops. He burned his papers and committed suicide by swallowing the cyanide pill with which all SOE agents were provided. He was just 21 years of age.

Letac and his brother returned to Brittany by sea on the night of 3/4 February, 1942. Unfortunately, when stopped and searched, the Germans found incriminating documents in their pockets. They were arrested, interrogated and tortured and were eventually committed to one of the notorious German concentration camps. Both survived the experience.

Daniel Cordier, a small and slightly built young man who had trained at Inchmery as a saboteur and at Thame Park as a radio operator, became one of the secretaries to Jean Moulin, General de Gaulle's chief political emisarry who ventured into and out of France on several occasions in his efforts to unite the various underground political and resistance factions. Moulin became the president of the underground National Council for Resistance. In June, 1943, the Gestapo pounced and caught the entire Council as it was assembling for a meeting at a house on the outskirts of Lyons. Cordier escaped but was now known to the Gestapo, i.e. 'burned', and was therefore of no further use as an agent. He managed to evade capture and remained in France for the rest of the war.

Altogether, twenty-eight radio operators who had received their secret agent training at Inchmery were parachuted into France in 1941 and 1942. Only Cordier and one other escaped arrest by the Germans. Of the twenty-six who were caught, nine were executed and sixteen were deported to German concentration camps after interrogation and torture. Among these was Louis Kerjean who survived the horrors of Buchenwald and Dachau and after the war rose to the rank of General in the French army. Another survivor of a Nazi concentration camp, also from Inchmery, was Georges Ledoux who was parachuted into France on 12 December, 1942.

One of the Inchmery-trained operators was Gerard Brault, who was twenty years of age. He was arrested by the Gestapo on 15 October, 1942, but was fortunate in being consigned to a French prison instead of a Gestapo gaol, from which, with the help of one of the warders, he managed to escape. He returned to Britain in July, 1943, having been on the run for nine months. On 11 April, 1944, he was again parachuted into France and went into the Ardennes to organize and run a 'maquis', a well-armed band of men fighting the Germans openly on the Belgian frontier. He was liberated by the Americans on 5 September, 1944.

French agents suffered appalling losses, especially during the early stages of the war, through inexperience of clandestine warfare and their own lack of security and their insistence on a centrally controlled underground organization under Jean Moulin. As a nation the French, perhaps more so than the British, were not conspiratorial by nature. They ignored the dangers of centralization at great cost to their resistance leaders and had none of the suspiciousness or the clandestine and conspiratorial skills of the Polish members of SOE, who used to tease them unmercifully about their inexperience.

The last word on the agents drawn from the original group of Free French parachutists at Inchmery House must be those of General Georges Berge, who in 1992 recounted that they were in the forefront, dropping from the sky in 1941 into action, following the SOE directives long before the (French) National Council for Resistance was formed. For a long time, he wrote, in 1941 and 1942 Station 36 remained the crucible where the first Intelligence and Action teams were formed.

The Free French forces vacated Inchmery House towards the end of 1942. Latterly it had become a 'Holding Station' for trained agents of SOE's RF Section awaiting transportation to France.

There is no record of the date on which the French left Inchmery, or where they went after they left. What is known is that at the end of 1942 or very early in 1943 a troop of the British Small Scale Raiding Force moved from Anderson Manor in Bere Regis in Dorset to Inchmery House. Because of the tight security surrounding every movement and event in those days, the SSRF team were totally unaware that the Free French had occupied the house, or that it had been a holding station for Free French secret agents. They were under the impression that the previous occupants had been a unit of the Lovat Scouts, part of Lord Lovat's commandos.

The Small Scale Raiding Force was also known as 62 Commando and was sometimes referred to by SOE as Station 62. It was one of a considerable number of small units formed by all three of our Armed Services early in the war to carry out specialized and often very risky tasks. Some of the better known of these units were David Stirling's SAS, Popski's Private Army, No. 10. Inter-Allied Commando, the Royal Marine Special

Boat Squadron and units of frogmen such as the Combined Operations Pilotage Parties.

As early as December, 1940, an informal agreement had been reached between SOE and Combined Operations Headquarters that SOE would handle small-scale raids on enemy territory by units of up to thirty men, ideally foreigners, so that if stranded during an operation they could melt into the countryside of their native countries and stand a better chance of escape. But the control of such operations did not for long remain exclusively with SOE and most were taken over by one or other of the Armed Services. However, SOE did retain control over the Small Scale Raiding Force until it was disbanded in April, 1943.

The SSRF was originally conceived in the winter of 1940, the brain-child of a member of SOE, Captain Gus March-Phillipps. In March, 1941, together with a young engineering graduate who had served as a Lieutenant in the Royal Army Service Corps, Geoffrey Appleyard, (the officer who rescued Captain Berge), he requisitioned a Brixham trawler, the *Maid Honor*, that had already been converted into a yacht, and had it refitted to look like a trawler but with a dummy superstructure to house hidden guns and other fittings to make it suitable for raiding purposes. It was afterwards based at Poole but the Admiralty made difficulties that prevented it from being used in home waters in the Channel.

However, an opportunity arose in West Africa. March-Phillipps and a crew of five distinguished themselves in what Nelson's navy would have described as a 'cutting out expedition', the hijacking of a 7,500-ton Italian cargo vessel, with a valuable cargo of iron ore, moored in neutral waters off the Spanish island of Fernando Po in the Gulf of Guinea. Its capture also prevented it from being used to re-supply German U-boats and surface raiders. Their success captured the imagination of Winston Churchill and the new chief of Combined Operations, Lord Louis Mountbatten, and on the return of the so-called '*Maid Honor* Force' to the United Kingdom the unit was encouraged to expand, in preparation for raids on the coast of Europe. The unit was re-named the Small Scale Raiding Force. Its base as at Anderson Manor in Bere Regis and in 1942, using a variety of Coastal Forces craft, mounted a whole series of daring raids along the coast of Europe and on the Channel Islands. Some of these raids were very successful and some were disastrous.

The SSRF was expanded from three to four Troops under the command of Lieutenant-Colonel Bill Stirling, brother of David Stirling, founder of the SAS. The newly raised D Troop, under the command of Colin Ogden-Smith, was located at Inchmery House where plans were being hatched for small boat raids using limpet mines on blockade-running enemy shipping. They were evidently unaware that an identical type of operation was carried out on Bordeaux during this period by the Royal Marines, the so-called 'Cockleshell Heroes', using canoes and limpet mines.

The Technical Officer and explosive expert for the proposed operation was Captain C.P. Wykeham-Martin of the Royal Engineers. He was also given the task of designing and building, in conjunction with Camper and Nicholson's of Gosport, several small raiding craft. The prototypes of these craft were hidden in a creek near Inchmery House.

In the spring of 1943 so many secret operations were going on along the coast of Europe that there was no opportunity for the SSRF to put its plans into effect. On 19 April it was decided that the SSRF should be disbanded. The men were returned to their units, mainly to No.12 Commando and their officers dispersed, some of them into other SOE units. Sadly, Colin Ogden-Smith was killed in action after being retrained as an SOE Jedburgh resistance co-ordinator and parachuted in uniform into France. And Geoffrey Appleyard, who had seen so much action before and during his time as second-in-command of the SSRF and who had ferried the two Free French agents out to the submarine *HMS Tigris* in bad weather, was killed in action in Sicily in March, 1943.

After the SSRF left Inchmery, the house was taken over by the Polish Sixth Bureau (Secret Service) for an unknown period, whether as an Intelligence headquarters, a holding station for agents awaiting transport, a specialist training centre or some other purpose is not known. During this period they were still sending a considerable number of men to be trained in the main Finishing School at Beaulieu.

Local rumour has it that the Poles were still at Inchmery during the run-up to D-Day in June, 1944. Another piece of evidence suggests that they may have been there until the late summer. In the stables of Inchmery House carved in Polish is the inscription 'God Help Us'. The Warsaw uprising occurred in August, 1944. It was utterly crushed by the Germans in September while the Russians looked on from the outskirts of the city watching the Germans destroy the Polish underground army which constituted a severe threat to the Communists' intended post-war occupation of Poland. They refused to allow the British or the Americans to support the Poles from airbases in their newly-conquered Polish territory. This forced the Allies to fly to Warsaw from a base in Italy, 900 miles away. Two hundred and forty tons of supplies were parachuted into Warsaw by the Allies in support of the Polish Home Army, and forty-one aircraft and their crews were lost in the process. The Poles and the Germans each lost over 10,000 men in the sixty-three days of bitter street fighting among the rubble and sewers of Warsaw.

No wonder the Poles at Inchmery pleaded to God for help.

Chapter V

THE PROFESSIONALS

When the Secret Intelligence Service refuses to co-operate, where do you find people to teach secret agents their clandestine skills, and who, then, decides what type of skills are necessary?

After the First World War Britain was almost alone among European nations in failing to acknowledge that Intelligence was a profession and suitable as a career for officers of our armed services. The Intelligence Corps, created during the First World War, had been disbanded in December, 1929. Regular officers with wartime experience in Intelligence had long been demobilized or returned to their regiments and many of the older and most experienced of them had retired. The three armed services had resumed their tradition of assuming that Intelligence was merely a matter of common sense, and were filling Intelligence staff appointments with officers shunted sideways for a stint of two years or less before continuing their normal careers up the command ladder.

By 1938 our military Intelligence services had been scandalously run down and were in a parlous state. Only a handful of dedicated regimental officers were serving in small Intelligence departments within the War Office. There were no plans for re-forming the Intelligence Corps and nobody foresaw the huge demands for Intelligence officers that were to be made by the creation of organizations such as SOE, the radio, cryptography, scientific and other Intelligence services. Somebody had drafted a plan to place Field Intelligence Officers in all military headquarters, but since nobody had been trained for the task and nobody had been earmarked for the appointments in the event of war, it was a useless piece of paper. It was discovered that there were only fifty former Intelligence Officers remaining on the Regular Army Reserve of Officers and all of them were now twenty years older than they had been when they were placed on the Reserve.

The 1922 edition of the *Manual of Military Intelligence* had recommended that businessmen, lawyers, bankers and other civilian professionals with language skills should be recruited for Intelligence work in the event of hostilities. This was used as a guide for recruiting people in 1938. A cry went out for volunteers with language skills and the 500 men who responded were placed on the Army Officers' Emergency Reserve. They were, of course, untrained in military affairs and military Intelligence and were invited to take a course lasting ten days at their own expense! They were called up in 1939.

That same year Major Gerald Templer, (later Field Marshal Sir Gerald) a staff officer in a Military Intelligence Directorate, was given the unenviable task of trying, in a matter of months, to repair the ravages of decades of neglect in order to meet the need for Intelligence officers for staff appointments and for manning a re-formed Intelligence Corps. As a result of his foresight and energetic action it was possible, but only just, to fill all the Field Intelligence appointments required for the British Expeditionary Force preparing to go to France at the outbreak of war.

The creation of SOE in July, 1940, suddenly confronted officers such as Gubbins and Holland, and their superiors in the Military Intelligence Directorate, with a need for the massive expansion of their manpower, and they, too, followed the recruiting recommendations of the old *Manual of Military Intelligence* to handle the administration of the new secret service. However, this famous, antiquated manual provided no guidance or advice on where to find people with experience to teach the clandestine arts and crafts to the proposed army of secret agents that SOE intended to recruit.

The Secret Intelligence Service, which nobody would admit existed, was also ineffective and badly run down and was in any case hostile to the whole SOE concept. Although it had its own training schools for spies, it was extremely reluctant to compromise its own administrative and training personnel, or to disclose its own operational methods, by training amateur agents who were bound to be caught by the Nazis and forced to talk about where and how they had been trained and by whom. The SIS really wanted nothing to do with SOE and had to be inveigled into allowing several of the staff of its unwanted foundling, Section D, to be transferred to SOE, including Guy Burgess, later to be joined by Kim Philby, at the age of 28, in pitiful ignorance that the pair of them had about five years' experience apiece as active spies of a foreign power, Russia! Neither of them was regarded by the authorities as having any experience of spying or of training spies!

The moment Colin Gubbins was appointed as head of Training and Operations in SOE in November, 1940, he got rid of Burgess whom he recognized as a drunken, homosexual rake and a security risk, but in the

The Plaque in the Bookcase (*Montagu Ventures Ltd*)

Special Training School (STS) 31: The Rings, HQ of the Finishing School.
Intelligence Corps Museum)

3. The House in the Woods, Officers' Mess for the School Staff. *(Intelligence Corps Museum)*

4. STS 35: The Vineyards, where many radio operators did their security training. *(Intelligence Corps Museum)*

TS 34: The Drokes, first used for the Spanish Republicans, and where many Norwegian and Polish agents were trained. *(Intelligence Corps Museum)*

TS 33: The House on the Shore, also first used by the Spaniards and favoured by the Poles. *(Intelligence Corps Museum)*

7. Part of STS 31, Hartford House was the smallest of all the houses and used for the very first students. *(Intelligence Corps Museum)*

8. STS 36: Boarmans was favoured by the French Section and was where the first intake of women agents were trained. *(Intelligence Corps Museum)*

nchmery House, BCRA agent training centre, later occupied by SOE's Small Scale aiding Force, then by the Polish 6th Bureau. *(C. Cunningham)*

Former RF Section agents and Special Forces personnel. *Left to right:* Georges Ledoux (see p. 41), Pierre Pradere, General Bourdis, General Kerjean (see p. 41), Marcel Sourez, Cornel Desrousseaux (ex SAS). *(Ron Hansford & Mme Alma Kerjean)*

11. Louis Kerjean in 1940. He wa later parachuted into France, captured by the Gestapo and imprisoned in both Buchenwal and Dachau.

12. He survived to become a General in the French Army. *(Both photographs: Ron Hansford and Mme Alma Kerjean)*

Lieutenant-Colonel S. H. C. Woolrych, OBE, Commandant of the Finishing School. *(Intelligence Corps Museum)*

14. Brigadier George Hill, one of the first instructors. *(Special Forces Clu*

15. Kim Philby *(standing)* and Paul Dehn, the Propaganda Warfare and Unattributable Sabotage Instructors, in the garden of The House in the Woods.
(Courtesy of Mrs Ann Sarell.)

light of subsequent events he clearly had no such qualms about Philby. The fact that the SIS had recruited a man as blatantly untrustworthy and lacking in security as Burgess, however good he may have been as an administrator or diplomat, (which is questionable) is adequate testimony of its appalling nepotism and lack of discernment and provides ample justification for Philby's scurrilous remarks about its professional incompetence.

The official records state that the syllabus of the Beaulieu course was based upon the training being given at the MI Wing at Lochailort (Arisaig) and at STS 17, i.e. Section D's clandestine training school at Brickendonbury Hall, for which Philby claims to have been instrumental in drawing up the syllabus at Burgess's instigation. Gubbins and his team had visited STS 17 to get ideas for the proposed new school at Beaulieu.

If Philby's autobiography is read carefully it is obvious that he had already received training from the Russians in a variety of spy tradecrafts. He was familiar with codes, cyphers and the use of secret inks, knew how to use a special camera for photographing documents and was experienced in caching his spying equipment. He was also skilled at shaking off anybody tailing him, skilled in the use of rudimentary and effective disguises and in making clandestine contacts, including the use of 'drops', i.e. leaving messages for others to collect from dead letter boxes. It is a matter of speculation as to how much of this knowledge he incorporated in his syllabus for the Brickendonbury course and how much of it, if any, ultimately filtered through to the Beaulieu course.

Evidently nobody at the time thought it appropriate to question him in detail about what qualifications he possessed for making proposals about the syllabus, the selection of trainees and security techniques. Neither did anybody bother to ask him where he had acquired his knowledge. All that is known for certain is that the Brickendonbury syllabus provided part of the blueprint for the Beaulieu course.

It is now well known that Philby became an agent for the French Comintern in the summer of 1933, at the age of 21. He had worked for a communist underground organization in Vienna in 1933 and '34 and had in fact organized an escape line from Vienna to Czechoslovakia for communists on the run from the Austrian authorities. In February, 1934, he had married one of the key underground organizers, Litzi Friedmann, a Comintern agent, to get her out of the country. His activities in Vienna had evidently been noted by the Soviet Russian secret service, the NKVD (the forerunner of the KGB), and in the spring of the same year he was recruited by an NKVD agent in England. All that is known about this recruiting agent is that he was not a Russian. Philby was later to complain that he was not given anything to do for the Russians during the next two years but careful reading of his autobiography and several biographies that mention this period of his life suggests that it was during these two years that he received some training from the Russians in various spy crafts, including coding and communications. One source said he received this training in Paris, another that it was in Spain where he made two trips with his wife, ostensibly on holiday, in 1934 and 1935, paid for by the Russians. He went to Spain again at their instigation in February, 1937, under the cover of a freelance journalist to report on the Civil War and spy on Franco's Nationalist forces for the opposing Communists and Republicans. He remained in Spain on Russian instructions until August, 1939, four months after the end of the Civil War. By that time he had become an accredited correspondent of *The Times*, an affiliation that was later to bring him into contact with many influential people who he eventually used to worm his way into secret service circles. On the outbreak of the Second World War *The Times* sent him as their accredited correspondent to the British Expeditionary Force Headquarters at Arras, and he was evacuated from Boulogne during the retreat in May, 1940.

In the early winter of 1940 Colin Gubbins invited Philby to prepare the syllabus for the Propaganda Warfare module of the Beaulieu course. His proposals were accepted and he was enlisted to teach it at Beaulieu.

Philby claims to have gained his knowledge of dirty techniques of propaganda warfare from talking to his acquaintances in the advertising business and learning from them the dirtiest tricks of their profession! He also claims to have made frequent visits to acquaintances working in the 'black' propaganda section of the Political Warfare Executive at Woburn Abbey to learn what he could from them. These visits brought him into contact with senior politicians from whom he acquired some knowledge of Britain's post-war political intentions, information which he says he passed on to the Russians.

One cannot help wondering how much of his knowledge of 'black' propaganda techniques was acquired not from Woburn or from his friends in the advertising business but from any training he may have received from the Russians or from reading communist handbooks for Party Organizers. The latter are full of dirty tricks for infiltrating and corrupting political organizations and inflaming the masses with half-truths and lies so outrageous that they cannot be proved or disproved.

He is reputed to have taken the ten-day agent training course at

Beaulieu before joining the staff, and is said to have been an exceedingly apt pupil! He must have been laughing up his sleeve at the floundering amateurism of these early courses. Afterwards his performance as the principal instructor on propaganda warfare was regarded by his superiors, his fellow instructors and his students as outstanding, even though he had a marked stammer and imbibed such enormous quantities of drink that his contemporaries marvelled that he could stay upright and deliver coherent lectures.

Philby admits that his posting to Beaulieu took him away from the centre of things and thwarted his activities as a Russian spy, so that out of frustration he took to drinking heavily. He also admits to using the excuse of visiting Woburn to get away from Beaulieu to make his clandestine contacts with the Russians. As a civilian he was not bound by military regulations regarding periods of leave, nor was he obliged to take his share of the routine military duties that tie serving officers to their bases out of working hours.

In the early autumn of 1941, almost a year after joining SOE, he was recruited into the Secret Intelligence Service's Section V, by a man he had met while working at Brickendonbury. He was transferred from the SOE to the SIS and was replaced at Beaulieu by Captain J. Hackett, seconded from the Political Warfare Executive at Woburn. Philby remained an active spy for the Russians until 1951, when he came under suspicion. He went to the Middle East as a journalist and occasional agent for the British Secret Service (even though he was strongly suspected) until he defected to Russia from Beirut on 27 January, 1963. He died in Moscow on 11 May, 1988, at the age of 76.

Two other individuals from Section D were also transferred to Beaulieu with Philby. One was Professor E.J. Patterson, the other was George Hill.

Eric Patterson was a fifty-year-old Manxman, a well known academic specializing in adult education who had somehow become a Secret Service specialist in codes, ciphers and secret inks. He had been educated in Germany in his youth, before going to Cambridge to read for his degree and afterwards, soon after the First World War, returned to Germany for post-graduate studies. He held a series of lectureships between the wars and travelled to Poland and Yugoslavia studying their systems of adult education. At the outbreak of the Second World War he was the Principal of Bonar Law College at Ashridge in Hertfordshire and during the early years of the war he was a member of the Advisory Council for Adult Education in HM Forces and served on other high level education committees. He left Beaulieu in the spring of 1941, replaced by an army officer, Ralph Vibert. In his memoirs, Vibert said he had paid visits to Liverpool to consult 'a great expert' on secret inks. During the war there was, apparently, a sub-department of Liverpool University known as the Testing and Code Facility that specialized in the chemistry of secret inks and possessed a laboratory which worked for the Liverpool headquarters of the Postal Censorship division of MI 5, chemically treating suspect overseas mail and passing it under ultra-violet lamps. Patterson is known to have been a lecturer at Liverpool University at one stage of his career, but it is not certain that he was the expert mentioned by Vibert.

George Hill was also in his late fifties and held the rank of major. Known to his colleagues at Beaulieu as 'Uncle', a term frequently used in service officers' messes for an officer well above the average age for his rank, he was in fact none other than the former Brigadier G.A. Hill, DSO, OBE, MC, who had been a very successful British spy in Russia during the First World War and one of a famous trio of British spies in Russia at that time, the other two being Paul Dukes and the fabulous Sidney Reilly.

Hill was the son of a British merchant who, early in the present century, had business interests spreading from Siberia to Persia (Iran). George had travelled extensively in this area with his father and learned to speak Russian well. He had spent the earlier years of the First World War in the Intelligence Corps before transferring to the Royal Flying Corps. He had been one of the first men ever to land a plane carrying secret agents behind enemy lines, in Bulgaria. He had been sent to Russia to join an RFC mission two months before the Bolshevik revolution. By the end of the war he had already done everything that the SOE agents would be required to do in the Second World War, and more.

Following the revolution and the Russo-German peace treaty of March, 1918, he became a sub-agent of the local Secret Service station chief, Ernest Boyce, whose duties involved working with the Bolsheviks on the one hand while on the other making mischief with, and spying upon, German Missions and troop movements in Russia. Hill claimed to have won the confidence of Trotsky and to have helped him to develop the Cheka (later the KGB). He also claimed that he had set up an Intelligence service in the Bolshevik army (later to become the Soviet Military Intelligence Service, the GRU) and trained them in the well-developed British technique of train-watching and how to identify German units in transit. He sent information on the troop movements by telegraph to London. He also taught the Russians how to intercept the mail of the German Missions in Petrograd and Moscow, and how to decode the intercepts.

Despairing of ever getting any real co-operation from the Bolsheviks he set up his own secret organization for monitoring German troop movements, operated his own secret courier service to convey his information back to England and created a special section of Czarist officers to work behind the German's lines, derailing German troop trains and supply trains, arming Russian peasants and inciting them to insurrection. Unfortunately for him, the Bolsheviks managed to penetrate this organization.

Later Hill linked up with Sidney Reilly in the latter's plot to disaffect the Lettish bodyguards of the Bolshevik leaders and use them to assassinate Lenin and the top Bolsheviks, an operation timed to coincide with an Allied landing of troops at Archangel to prevent Allied war materials and shipping from falling into German hands. The coup came unstuck in August, 1918, when other people with similar ideas but different motives for bumping off Lenin and his associates, beat them to it and made a hash of it. The head of the Petrograd Cheka was assassinated and Dora Kaplan, an extreme left-winger, shot and severely wounded Lenin, unleashing a reign of terror. The British were blamed by the Bolsheviks, the British Embassy was stormed, the naval attaché was shot and killed and Robert Bruce Lockhart, a British diplomat, was arrested and subsequently became the victim of the first ever Soviet attempt, made by a Cheka interrogator by the name of Peters, to brainwash a foreigner. The Secret Serviceman, Ernest Boyce, for whom Hill worked, was arrested and Reilly and Hill were driven underground to escape arrest. Eighteen of Hill's secret couriers and agents were caught and shot by the Cheka.

Hill, Bruce Lockhart, and the imprisoned Boyce, were eventually released via a diplomatic swap, but on reaching Finland Hill was ordered to go back into Russia on a sabotage mission, which he carried out very successfully. Philby said that Hill was the only man he had ever met who had actually sabotaged trains by pouring sand into their axle boxes. Experiments by SOE during the Second World War proved that this method of sabotage was ineffective!

Hill was the only one of the original Beaulieu teaching team who had actually been a spy (excluding Philby), had experience of living the underground life of a secret agent and had survived to tell the tale. We do not know what subjects he taught. Not long after he joined the staff at Beaulieu, Winston Churchill, in a puckish mood, sent him back to Russia, to Moscow, with a small team of Beaulieu-trained officer-agents, to act as the senior SOE liaison officer with the Russian Secret police, the NKVD, who were well aware of his impeccable credentials! According to

Philby, the SOE liaison team's offices were thoroughly bugged, i.e. fitted with monitoring microphones, by the NKVD.

Philby's comments on the choice of staff at Beaulieu are worth recounting. He remarked that experienced secret service officers were in desperately short supply and of course could only have been obtained from the Secret Intelligence Service, which was hostile to the whole idea of SOE. Philby opines that had the SIS been asked to supply suitable instructors it would have off-loaded its duds, and had it done so it would have produced results too awful to contemplate. In the event, the denial of experienced SIS instructors forced SOE to find its own instructors from its own resources. Subsequent experience convinced Philby that in the circumstances the choice of raw instructors was wise, since the men chosen as instructors for the new school had more than their fair share of intelligence and imagination. He considered that they made the old hands look asinine!

His assumption that the first batch of instructors at Beaulieu were totally inexperienced in the task of training spies is largely correct, but with one very important exception.

The man chosen by Lieutenant-Colonel J.W. Munn, the first Commandant at Beaulieu, as his Chief Instructor was Major S.H.C. Woolrych, the Chief Instructor of the FS Wing of the Intelligence Training Centre at Matlock in Derbyshire. Woolrych was close on fifty years of age, was rather short and thick-set in stature, nearly bald and a veteran of the First World War. He claimed that he had security in his bones, and Philby was evidently very uneasy in his company for obvious reasons and described him as 'a nuisance', probably because he was too inquisitive for Philby's comfort. Six months after the school was set up he replaced Munn as the Commandant and remained in that post, except for one brief interlude, for the rest of the war.

Stanley Woolrych was a dark horse. He was an old spycatcher and spymaster, a gamekeeper turned poacher, whose activities in the First World War were to be repeated in the Second World War. The story of his career is a history of the Intelligence Corps and two of its principal activities: Field Security and military secret service work.

Born in Blackheath, London, in 1891, he was one of a large family and had four brothers and two sisters. His father was the headmaster of a local school who lost his job when the lease of the school ran out. He took his family to the Continent where the cost of living was cheaper and settled for a time in Chamonix in the French Alps close to the Italian frontier where the young Woolrychs learned to speak French fluently. They moved to Switzerland where Stanley became equally fluent in Swiss German. He was sent back to England, to be educated at Marlborough School, but his family's financial circumstances did not permit him to move on to university. Instead, he obtained a job with an insurance company and later with the West India Committee.

Soon after the outbreak of the First World War, at the age of 23 and already fluent in French and German, he visited the War Office and volunteered his services as an interpreter to the British Expeditionary Force. He was told to go home and wait for a reply which, when it arrived, informed him that no interpreters were needed because they were being provided by the French. However, the Army was starting a new thing called 'Intelligence'. Was he interested? When he replied that he was, he was called for a cursory examination of his knowledge of French and German and was subsequently called up in October, 1914, and posted to a motorcycle battalion in Putney. Here he was taught to ride a machine and to map-read and make reconnaissances of the local topography and write reports.

He was commissioned into the General Service Corps (and later transferred to the Intelligence Corps) early in November, 1914, and a month later he was posted, via GHQ St Omer, to the Western Front, to the 7th Division of the 4th Corps. He found himself almost a supernumerary and spent much of his time following up scare reports of alleged spies signalling to each other within the British lines, all of which had reasonable and innocuous explanations. Through these investigations he became known as 'the Divisional Spy'.

On Christmas Day, 1914, there was an unofficial armistice and the young Woolrych walked across the battlefield to the enemy trenches to talk to the German troops in their own language.

In January, 1915, he was ordered to draw panoramas of the whole of the mile-and-a-half Divisional front line and the opposing enemy trenches and terrain. It was one of the routine tasks given to Intelligence officers in the earlier years of the war and kept him occupied for some time. It took him into elevated positions already in use as observation posts by the Forward Observation Officers of the artillery, usually located in derelict buildings close to the firing line, the regular targets of enemy snipers and heavier guns. Many of his panoramas are currently held in the Intelligence Corps museum and indicate an exceptional eye for detail.

During a trip back to France by ferry after a spell of leave, a Belgian passenger sitting next to him told him that German troop trains were passing the foot of his garden. Were the British interested? On reporting the incident to his superiors he was sent to repeat his story to Divisional headquarters and so started the idea of train-watching as a source of military Intelligence on the enemy's order of battle.

On his return to the battle area he recognized a need to do something more than draw panoramas of the terrain to produce useful information on which to base tactical offensives. He began to work among the local population, especially those recently displaced from areas now occupied by the Germans, collecting from them topographical information and pre-war postcards of the areas. He also began interrogating enemy prisoners of war for the same sort of information and was able to use all this data to elaborate on the information in his panoramas. It was to earn him a mention in dispatches.

At the end of 1915 he was transferred from what the army called Intelligence (a) work to Intelligence (b) work, from collecting tactical Intelligence to secret service and counter-espionage work. He was posted to Folkestone to work with Major B.A.Wallinger who occupied an office in the Marine Parade overlooking the harbour. All the cross-channel ferries from Holland docked at Folkestone. Holland was a neutral country and a happy hunting ground for spies working for all the belligerent nations, and the ferries were carrying both agents and couriers. Wallinger and his staff of about five other officers, including Woolrych, recruited people from among the continental passengers and trained them to gather military intelligence, especially Order of Battle intelligence on the disposition of German units. The agents had to be trained to recognize German army uniforms and badges, as well as military formations, and learn how to transmit this information to their British controllers by a variety of means, including the use of secret inks to send messages by post and by carrier pigeons.

The total number of agents of this type operated by the British army in Europe during the First World War was astonishingly large, about 6,000, of whom nearly 700 were caught by the Germans. One hundred of them were shot and the rest imprisoned.

It was in the Folkestone office that Woolrych said he learned the rudiments of the spy trade, which was to stand him in good stead for his job in SOE some twenty-five years later.

In 1916 he was posted to Paris to set up a recruiting office and a school to teach Belgian refugees from German-occupied territories to spy on German troop movements. There were communities of re-settled Belgians scattered all over France and Woolrych, in civilian clothes and working under an assumed name, went from one to the other looking for recruits.

They were sent to the school in Paris where they were taught to recognize German units and German trains carrying the units to the Western Front. They were also taught the badges and insignia of various German units; Woolrych introduced three wooden tailor's dummies dressed in German uniforms (an idea he was later to introduce at Beaulieu). The next part of their training was to teach them train-watching, to note the time that the train passed the watching post and to identify the composition of the train, noting the type and number of the different types of carriages. On the walls of the school were diagrams of German trains of different lengths and various types of carriages. Some of these diagrams are among the papers left by Colonel Woolrych to the Intelligence Corps museum.

The agents were taught to recruit the services of their families to maintain a 24-hour watch on German troop movements and to write their reports on the thinnest and toughest tissue paper they could find, using a magnifying glass, mapping pens and Indian ink. The message could then be rolled into a tiny package and secreted about the human body or attached to a carrier pigeon. Some of these reports are also among the papers left by Woolrych to the Intelligence Corps museum.

Woolrych was later to write in his memoirs of the First World War:-

'The crux of all agent training is how the reports are to be transmitted. In the First World War we had to depend on written reports and ways of getting them out [to their controllers]. There had always been whole families of 'passeurs', that is, smugglers, living on the Dutch/Belgian frontier, who had immemorial methods of crossing the frontiers. For a time we pressed them into service but gradually the Germans closed all the loopholes and wired the frontier with electric fencing. Every kind of method was employed to circumvent the electrified wire.'

The agents were given rubber gloves, but some of them were electrocuted to death. Some used barrels with no tops or bottoms which were thrust through the wire to provide a tunnel to crawl through. Others crawled into beetfields, concealed their message in a beet and threw it over the wire to an accomplice on the Dutch side. A number of agents relied on carrier pigeons.

He continued his recruiting and training of spies for the better part of a year before he fell ill and was taken to hospital with appendicitis. He never returned to agent-running and was transferred to security duties with an inter-allied mission. Early in 1918, now a captain, he was posted back to the Western Front as chief Intelligence (b) officer to the Second Army under Stewart Menzies, who became chief of the British Secret Intelligence Service in 1939.

Woolrych was made responsible for Field Security (counter-espionage) work for the Second Army front. It was in this job that he used his knowledge of spies and spying to set up a counter-espionage organization comprising several subalterns and fifty 'Intelligence Police', called 'green-caps' because they wore green capcovers to distinguish them from the ordinary Military Police who wore red capcovers. The system he devised for policing a huge area became a model for Field Security operations during the Second World War. He divided his area of responsibility into sections of approximately 50 square miles and settled his policemen, who were linguists, in pairs and in plain clothes in each of these sectors and instructed them to get to know their areas intimately and make friends with the local population. He issued his men with questionnaires to make sure that they carried out their work diligently. He was thus able to monitor all movements and events, especially unusual events in the back areas of the Second Army front.

After the armistice, Woolrych, now a Major, moved with the army of occupation into Germany, where he set up the same system for monitoring events in the area for which he was responsible. He was demobilized in December, 1919, and placed on the Army's Special List.

He had married during the war and had a family. Between the wars he struggled to make a living as an import-export agent. He started his business with one of his brothers, who lived in Copenhagen, importing hosiery, but the business failed. He found another partner and began importing fashioned silk stockings, something that had not previously been available in this country. Woolrych acted as an agent between the manufacturers on the continent and the wholesale houses in this country. It provided him with a reasonable living until a tax was imposed upon silk, which ruined his business. He turned to importing Swiss woollen goods. In running his businesses he had learned a smattering of Danish and Norwegian. In his spare time he had a passionate interest in luxury liners and would take his sons down to the London docks for a treat to look at them. He was a keen amateur photographer and developed his own films. He was also an accomplished classical pianist and endeavoured to get an hour's practice at the piano every day. He even managed to do this during the Second World War when circumstances permitted, especially at Beaulieu where there was a grand piano in the officers' mess at The House in the Wood.

He was recalled to the colours on 2 September, 1939, only one day before war was declared. He was not one of the very small band of former Intelligence officers on the regular army officers reserve. He was given the rank of Captain on the General List (which was dubbed 'Cross and Blackwell's Own'), and made second-in-command of the Field Security Wing of the Military Police depot at Mychett in Surrey. With a staff of three captains, three sergeants, two corporals and five ATS girls, he set about re-forming the Field Security service. Since the Intelligence Corps had not yet been re-formed, the Army had reverted to the 1914 practice which regarded Field Security personnel as a branch of the Military Police.

The FS Wing at Mychett had the task of training volunteers with foreign language skills in a variety of FS duties, including rudimentary interrogation techniques, general security, how to keep security records and how to collect information on the enemy Order of Battle. They were then formed into standard Field Security units, teams comprising one officer, one senior NCO and thirteen sergeants and junior NCOs.

In April, 1940, the FS Wing moved to Sheerness on the Isle of Sheppey at the mouth of the River Thames opposite Southend. Heavy enemy bombing of the area soon forced it to move to Winchester where the King Alfred Teacher Training College was requisitioned to accommodate 200 or so trainees who were entering their basic pre-Intelligence training at regular intervals. It was while the depot was located at Winchester, in December, 1940, that the FS Wing of the Corps of Military Police became part of the newly re-formed Intelligence Corps.

The demand for Intelligence personnel grew at such a rapid rate that by October, 1942, the premises had become inadequate and the recruit depot moved to an enormous country house at Wentworth, near Rotherham in Yorkshire. The Winchester depot and later the Wentworth depot were basic training establishments for Other Ranks entering the Corps; officer recruits were sent for their basic training to either Pembroke or Oriel Colleges at Oxford, which had been requisitioned for the purpose.

The first Intelligence Training Centre, later renamed the School of Military Intelligence, was set up in Minley Manor near Camberley in 1939. In May, 1940, it moved into two hotels in Swanage and three months later, in August, it moved again, to Smedley's Hydro in Matlock, Derbyshire, and remained there until the end of the war. It was here that officers and men underwent their training for a variety of Intelligence duties.

Woolrych was recruited into SOE as the Chief Instructor for the proposed school at Beaulieu in January or February, 1941. He was a man of exquisite manners, a practising Christian, an accomplished linguist and a meticulous administrator. He was sufficiently tough-minded to have no qualms about training people, men and women, to be spies, and after he became Commandant had little hesitation in sacking any member of his staff whom he considered to be inadequate for the job. He got rid of several members of the team he had inherited from Munn.

During his time at Beaulieu he had to cope with a stream of visiting top brass from SOE, also foreign dignitaries and politicians, and many of our own politicians, including Hugh Dalton and Ernest Bevin. He disliked Dalton who had a habit of draping his arm over the shoulder of the person to whom he was speaking. But he enjoyed entertaining Bevin as a dinner guest. On one occasion he teased Bevin about the Labour Party's avowed intention of abolishing public schools. Bevin replied, 'Do you think we are crazy? Where else do you think we will get educated Ministers!'

After the war, at the age of fifty-five, he joined the Foreign Office to start its Information Department, a job which brought him into contact with many Ministers, including Denis Healey, who befriended him. The job took him to Strasbourg, to the Council of Europe, where he had many happy reunions with his former foreign friends and acquaintances in SOE. He retired in 1950 and died in 1983 at the age of ninety-two.

It was at Smedley's Hydro that he began looking for people to take with him to Beaulieu to instruct secret agents.

Chapter VI

THE 'PRETTY ODD FISH'

There were about sixteen officers on the teaching staff of the Beaulieu Finishing School. This figure does not include the School's administrative staff or the six residential adjutant 'housemasters' who also undertook some of the supervision of field exercises. Nor does it include visiting speakers, or the Conducting Officers seconded from the Country Sections to act as interpreters and confidants to each batch of trainee agents. It also excludes the trained agents seconded to the School after completing a tour of secret service, to pass on their up-to-date knowledge of the life and the hazards of working in enemy-occupied territories.

It was this motley collection of instructors, administrators and resting agents, all of them fluent in at least one foreign language and some in two or three, that led Philby to describe them as 'pretty odd fish'.

Very few of the staff of whatever rank remained at Beaulieu throughout the war. Almost all of them moved on to other jobs within SOE or returned to the regiments from which they had been borrowed and were replaced by others. However, it has been possible to identify over thirty officers who served on the instructor staff at various stages of the war. After the war at least eleven of them had distinguished careers in a very wide variety of occupations ranging from business and the film and theatre industries, commerce, stockbroking, the manufacture of pottery, academia, the diplomatic service, the law and one became a distinguished couturier.

They were, as Philby remarked, a pretty odd lot and included a burglar. And they were teaching some pretty rum subjects, the like of which would have been more suited to the criminal sub-culture of Wormwood Scrubs, where, behind the backs of the warders, hardened criminals would probably have passed such knowledge by word of mouth to first-time offenders! The curriculum included such subjects as murder, arson, train-wrecking and other forms of sabotage, robbery, safe-breaking and key-making, burglary and housebreaking, forgery and 'black' propaganda, blackmail, false pretences and 'casing' premises, all of which were unlikely topics for army officers to be teaching as part of a curriculum of an authorized training course. Indeed, the German counter-espionage agencies called Beaulieu 'the Gangster School'.

The majority of the instructors were recruited from the Intelligence Corps and came into SOE on the 'old boy network', mainly via the School of Military Intelligence, although some visiting speakers were on loan from Scotland Yard's burglary squad and from MI 5.

The recruitment of staff for Beaulieu had been started at the end of 1940 by Gubbins and Munn. Major S.H.C. Woolrych had been earmarked for the job of Chief Instructor early in 1941, and he, in turn, approached four members of his teaching staff at the Intelligence Training Centre at Matlock saying, 'I've got something important to tell you chaps.' He disclosed that he had been recruited into SOE and was looking for people to take with him to Beaulieu.

The four members of the staff, all captains, were Leslie Charley, about whom very little more is known except that he became a Lieutenant-Colonel in SOE, 'Bill' Brooker, Cuthbert Skilbeck and John (later Sir John) Wedgwood, of the famous pottery family. Skilbeck, who died in June, 1996, related that Woolrych picked on Brooker because he knew Brooker's parents, and that he, Skilbeck, and John Wedgwood were Brooker's close friends. All three of them were of a similar age. Brooker and Skilbeck were 32, Wedgwood a couple of years older. Woolrych had known Leslie Charley during the First World War.

During the course of the war Brooker, Skilbeck and Wedgwood were to succeed Woolrych in the role of Chief Instructor at Beaulieu but it was John Wedgwood who, according to official records, held the post for the longest period, two years, before handing over in June, 1944, to the last Chief Instructor, Peter Folliss.

R.M. Brooker (always known as Bill) was by far the most colourful of the four, a rumbustious extrovert who had a meteoric rise to the rank of Lieutenant-Colonel within SOE until he fell out with Gubbins over the direction SOE was taking in the selection and training of secret agents. Brooker, who had no operational experience, but was probably basing his ideas on the experience of the Free French and the Poles, favoured the recruitment of Europeans already in place in enemy occupied territories. SOE initially had no trained secret agents and therefore had been forced to use commandos until it had trained inexperienced civilians who in the early 1940s had been readily caught by the Nazis. As the war progressed it showed a distinct preference for seasoned service personnel wearing their uniforms and acting in a para-military capacity. There was a head-on clash of egos which ultimately resulted in Brooker being demoted and shunted to one side where he could do no harm, to the job of a Conducting Officer to Americans training in SOE's schools, including Beaulieu. But not before he had distinguished himself in Canada and in the United States as an authority on agent training, even though he had spent only nine months on the Beaulieu instructor staff and had only eighteen months of war service altogether. This may seem little to qualify him as an expert, but in wartime, in his field, expertise was counted in months rather than in years.

After the war he built himself a successful career in the travel business, at one time becoming the controlling shareholder and Managing Director of the Henry Lunn travel firm. He launched several other enterprises which were bought out. In 1954 he retired briefly to Montreux where he started up another enterprise. He retired again in New York but was enticed out of retirement to work in the hotel industry for two very well known organizations, a job which took him around the world. By the time he finally retired in 1977, at the age of 68, he was the co-founder of the Association of British Travel Agents and had served on ABTA's first council. He died in January, 1995, at the age of eighty-six.

Brooker was a large man; some said he had the stature of King Henry VIII. He was a born salesman and a brilliant and convincing lecturer with an immense fund of stories that he could tell in his first language, which was French. Philby described him as 'the cleverest man I have ever met in my life'.

Bill Brooker was born in Paris in 1909, the son of the Manager of Thomas Cook's Paris Office. He had worked for a while for a merchant in Mincing Lane in the City of London before joining Nestlé's at their headquarters in Vevey in Switzerland. Throughout the 1930s he had travelled extensively across Europe selling Nestlé's products and was in Barcelona at the outbreak of the Spanish Civil War in the late summer of 1936. He had to leave in a hurry and at the age of 27 he was notably successful in smuggling the Company's blocked pesetas out of Spain over the Pyrenees, using couriers and clandestine routes and, to quote his words, 'volumes of false papers and plenty of imagination'. This was his only experience of clandestine operations, although at Beaulieu and in North America he always gave the deliberate impression of having had extensive operational experience as a secret agent.

He and Cuthbert Skilbeck formed a highly successful partnership which was to last until March, 1943. Between them they can fairly claim to have been the midwifes not only of the courses run at Beaulieu, but they also played a significant role in setting up and running courses at SOE's Canadian school known as Camp X in Oshawa, just outside Toronto on the shores of Lake Ontario. Together they were the architects of several courses that were eventually to be run by the Office of Strategic Services, the OSS, the American equivalent of SOE. Indeed, Brooker played a very significant role in bringing OSS into being and had enormous influence with the American General William (Wild Bill) Donovan, the founder of the modern American Secret Service, the Central Intelligence Agency. Brooker played a dominant role in shaping the OSS training programme during the latter half of 1942. He and Skilbeck also designed courses run by the American Central Intelligence Agency. One of these was for training agents for clandestine security operations all over South America.

Cuthbert Skilbeck had lived in Paris and Dresden during his teens and had afterwards returned to this country and joined the 500-year-old family firm of drysalters (merchants for raw chemicals, dyes and gums) which he rejoined after the war. He was fluent in French and German and in his younger days could speak a smattering of Norwegian, which he had acquired while staying at a little house his father had owned in Norway.

John Wedgwood had been educated at Winchester and Oxford and had spent three years on the continent before joining the family pottery business and becoming one of its directors four years before the outbreak of the war. He is frequently described as being notoriously 'absent-minded', or vague, dreamy and eccentric, characteristics which concealed a penetrating intellect. One of the Beaulieu secretaries described him as 'delightful but vague' and relates that on one occasion he was preparing his lecture notes in the garden of The Rings but failed to notice that his finished sheets were being blown away. Some of the office staff ran out into the garden to rescue them. Philby described him as 'pale and wide-eyed and would break long silences by unexpected and devastating sallies'. One of his colleagues described him as 'a very engaging, whimsical character'. His eccentricity was an example of what Philby meant when he described the staff at Beaulieu as 'pretty odd fish'.

It is most unlikely that Wedgwood was in fact clinically 'absent-minded'; it is far more likely that, like many so-called absent-minded professors, he was notoriously inattentive when confronted with matters that he found trivial or uninteresting and was apt to drift into profound mental pre-occupation with matters that he considered to be more challenging. He left Beaulieu in June, 1944, to take up the post of Military Intelligence Staff Officer with the Fifth North Staffordshire Regiment and subsequently served in the Arctic and in Italy. After the war he returned to the family pottery organization and became its deputy chairman and roving ambassador. At one period he tried, unsuccessfully, to enter politics. He was a noted mountaineer and caver and a keen walker. He died in 1989 at the age of 82.

All three of them had answered appeals in the newspapers for foreign-language speakers and had been called up and posted as privates into the Field Security Police at the Corps of Military Police depot at Mychett. One of their instructors was Captain S.H.C. Woolrych.

On completion of their initial training they were promoted to the rank of Lance Corporal. Brooker and Skilbeck were sent on a Sergeant Instructor's course at Mychett and after serving as sergeant-instructors for a few months they were commissioned as second lieutenants in the General List in February, 1940, and were put in charge of Field Security Sections. Wedgwood was also soon commissioned.

Brooker was posted to a Section working in the docks at Tyneside and Skilbeck was sent to take charge of a half-Section in the docks at Marseilles. Their jobs, in both cases, were to screen the crews of ships entering the docks, to try and ensure that none of the seamen were working in clandestine capacities for the Germans or the Italians. In this job they learned to interrogate in a foreign language and learned the art and difficulties of interrogating without any sophisticated aids save their own wiliness.

After the fall of France the Germans quickly occupied the northern part of the country but were slow to exert a controlling influence over the Vichy administration of the south of France. Skilbeck and very many other British service personnel were able to get away from the continent weeks after the defeat of the British Expeditionary Force and its evacuation from the beaches of Dunkirk at the end of May, 1940. Skilbeck left France at the end of June and by a circuitous sea route returned to England, to the depot at Sheerness, on 10 July, 1940, and was reunited with Brooker and many other friends. When he arrived at his home his wife grumbled about him taking so long to get home after the fall of France, and he had retorted that he was 'bloody lucky to have got home at all considering the situation in France, after running the gauntlet of German submarines in the Mediterranean and the Atlantic, and sailing half way to America in a shipping convoy to avoid them!'

When the Intelligence Corps recruit centre was created at Winchester, Brooker and Skilbeck moved there for a brief period before transferring to the Intelligence Training Centre at Smedley's Hydro at Matlock to teach on the officers' and OR's Field Security courses. Here they met up with John Wedgwood and with Stanley Woolrych, now a major and the chief instructor of Field Security training. Also on Woolrych's staff was Lieutenant Malcolm Muggeridge.

Brooker, Skilbeck, Wedgwood and, possibly, Leslie Charley arrived together at Beaulieu in March or April, 1941, and only then were they confronted with the task of designing syllabuses.

The general outline of the content of agent training had already been the subject of discussions between Colin Gubbins, 'Jimmy' Munn and Stanley Woolrych, and by the time Brooker, Skilbeck and Wedgwood arrived at Beaulieu several courses had already been run by Hill, Philby and a number of other unknown tutors. Munn and Woolrych had, according to Cuthbert Skilbeck, 'already laid on people to teach specialist subjects like codes and secret inks'. This suggests that Gubbins and the senior training staff had already decided upon a modular format for the Beaulieu courses, that is, had decided to prepare a number of self-contained packages or modules, each of variable length and complexity, to provide sufficient flexibility to enable them to tailor courses of a mixed bag of topics to meet whatever demands would be made by the Country Sections for superficial or in-depth training of agents of various sorts. There were at least seven modules, Agent Management, Enemy Organizations and their functions, Communications and Codes, Security and Resistance to Interrogation, Criminal Skills including railway sabotage, Propaganda Warfare and Black Propaganda, and Fieldcraft and Living Off the Land, i.e. survival training.

The content of some of these modules had been left to Woolrych to decide, and he delegated the detailed work to various members of the instructor staff. He left Brooker and Skilbeck to work out the details of the Security module. They shared a room at The Rings and spent very many hours discussing, often long into the night, which topics should be included. According to Skilbeck, 'We took the old *Manual of Military Intelligence* and, so to speak, stood it on its head, that is, we reversed what it said in the Field Security section about security against spying. The Beaulieu course was based upon our original two-week FS course.'

This is a gross simplification. The old *Manual of Military Intelligence* is nothing more than a series of pamphlets of pocket-book size held together at their bindings by Treasury Tags, two pairs of metal tags at the ends of two pieces of string, rather like very short bootlaces. Each pamphlet is described as a Section. The first three Sections concern the collection of military Intelligence by using the resources of the army, navy and air force, e.g. by skirmishing and patrolling, naval interception and air reconnaissance. The next two sections, Sections 4 and 5, the ones used by Brooker and Skilbeck, concern Counter Intelligence and Military Security, and Civil Security and Counter Espionage. Each Section is divided into chapters which lay down the general principles of Counter-Intelligence (e.g. physical measures to stop leakages of information, such as guarding premises, movement control, vetting etc) and Counter-Espionage (covert investigation and shadowing suspected persons, working with MI 5, etc). MI 5 obviously possessed valuable knowledge, based on its own operations, of what countermeasures the German security services would be likely to take and this could be reversed to teach potential agents how to avoid them. A fourth chapter concerns the organization of sources of information and records. This was of direct practical use for training agents on how to recognize unknown contacts and how to disguise their appearances by reversing, that is to say falsifying, many of the thirty visible characteristics of suspected persons which FS personnel were advised to observe and record.

In short the *Manual of Military Intelligence* provided Brooker and Skilbeck only with the bare bones of a syllabus for training and they had to rack their brains and imaginations for days and maybe for weeks to flesh it out. They were no doubt assisted by John Wedgwood and held frequent discussions with Woolrych. They gave the job of developing lectures and demonstrations on disguises and falsification of appearances to Peter Folliss.

Peter Folliss is something of an enigma. He was 26 years of age when the war broke out and he had followed the usual route into the Intelligence Corps Centre. He had received much of his Intelligence training from Brooker and Skilbeck while they were acting as instructors at Sheerness or Winchester earlier in the war. He is said to have been something of a misfit, cognitively, with the other original instructors, who tended to regard him as a callow youth. There is a rumour that Folliss came into SOE as a trained agent, via the Secret Intelligence Service, but this is unlikely in view of his known history of training at the Intelligence Training Centre. He may, however, have been an SIS contact with the school. He certainly moved from Beaulieu in 1946, by which time he was Chief Instructor, transferred to the SIS to set up a Special Training School for them near Gosport in Hampshire. When he died in 1970, at the age of 57, in New York, he had become the chairman of the board of an international company of high financiers.

Folliss was a Lieutenant in the Intelligence Corps when he arrived at Beaulieu in the spring of 1941 and he was one of the very few instructors to spend the entire war there. He rose from being a very junior member of the staff to the post of Chief Instructor which he took over in June, 1944, with the rank of Major. He was careful with his appearance and was slightly effete and languid, which people who knew him thought to be a pose, and gave rise to the rumour that he had been an actor, albeit a little-known one. He certainly encouraged people to draw this conclusion. He is said to have received some training in make-up from the Max Factor organization, whether before joining the forces or in preparation for his role at Beaulieu is not known.

Another member of the original Beaulieu staff who played a major role in developing agent training was Paul Dehn who, as well as being an outstanding and unforgettable lecturer on propaganda warfare, is credited with having masterminded and developed many of the ingenious practical exercises of the Beaulieu courses, the so-called Schemes.

Dehn's post-war reputation as a writer, scriptwriter, poet, film critic, opera librettist and song writer has vastly overshadow his wartime achievements, to the extent that when he died at the end of September 1976, at the early age of 63, no mention was made in his obituaries of the very significant part that he had played during the war years in SOE in this country and in Canada and America.

Dehn's work as a screenplay writer, but not his name, is well known to millions of people all over the world. He wrote the screenplays of a long list of well-known and award-winning films such as Goldfinger, Murder on the Orient Express, Orders to Kill, Seven Days to Noon, The Spy Who Came In From The Cold and many others. He was a sparkling performer who amused and entertained wherever he went both during the war and afterwards.

He was born in 1912, the son of a prosperous Manchester cotton merchant of Jewish descent. He was educated at Shrewsbury and Oxford and his godfather, the well-known drama critic James Agate, inspired him to take up writing. He became a film critic for a Sunday newspaper and also worked for a time as a journalist. He had a talent for foreign languages and was recruited into SOE at the age of 28 via the Intelligence Corps. He is said to have served for a time as Gubbins' personal assistant before joining the staff of Beaulieu some time before September, 1941. He was assigned to the task of teaching propaganda warfare and 'black' propaganda, along with Kim Philby who claims to have produced the draft curriculum of this module. Dehn specialized in this subject for the rest of his wartime career. He made an enormous impression on everybody with whom he came into contact both as an entertainer, 'A bloody

70

good night club act', and as a serious thinker with a warm and romantic nature. The official history of SOE describes him as having 'a vivid imagination and a rollicking sense of humour'. The official American history of the OSS described him thus: 'one of the finest lecturers to grace a classroom . . . Listening to him was better than reading the most exciting spy novel.' Another of his acquaintances commented, 'There was far more to Dehn than a quick wit, a piano and a packet of cigarettes. He was a first rate instructor, outstandingly good.' He had a powerful imagination, great sensitivity and strongly developed linguistic gifts. There is a famous story of how he sat in his bath learning by rote a Polish translation of his lecture. He eventually delivered it in perfect Polish to a group of Polish student agents who, afterwards, could not understand why he needed an interpreter to translate into English the questions they put to him!

Indeed he sparkled throughout his war career, in this country and in North America when, in the winter of 1942, he was posted as Chief Instructor, at Skilbeck's request, to Camp X at Oshawa in Canada. In the summer of 1943 he spent most of his time in America teaching propaganda warfare to members of the Office of Strategic Services. He was even well-known by proxy to the German counter-espionage agencies, because of the unforgettable impression he made on all the agents with whom he came into contact while they were undergoing training. After the German surrender he was sent to Norway on an interrogation mission and finished his service in SOE by compiling an agent handbook. When he died in 1976, a bachelor, he was deservedly described as one of the most versatile writers of his generation.

Another of the Beaulieu instructors who followed Brooker, Skilbeck and Dehn to Camp X in Canada was Captain Howard Burgess. He went there in May, 1942, and in the middle of a lecture he was delivering on security he broke off to ask the class if they had noticed a flash of lightning and then collapsed to the floor. He died from a stroke. He was twenty-six years of age.

One of the first instructors in codes, ciphers and secret inks was Ralph Vibert, a 29-year-old Jersey barrister, who, after the war, became a very prominent Jerseyman and a Commissioner of the Royal Court of Jersey. At the outbreak of hostilities he had been living in England with his family and as a civilian he had been recruited by an unspecified organization, probably an offshoot of GCHQ, to train as a cryptographer. After struggling for six months to learn this very difficult subject, one of a group of sixty trainees, fifty-seven of them, including Vibert, were rejected; only three of them made the grade and were probably sent to Bletchley Park, the main Government cryptography centre. However, because he could speak French and had mastered the art of coding, he was passed on to SOE. He was given a commission in the General List and sent to Beaulieu to teach coding and secret inks. He also used his barrister's interrogatory skills to exercise students' resistance to interrogation. He was soon joined by another expert in coding, thought to have been Captain D.C.Benn, and later by Captain P.B.(Pip) Whittaker, who, like Peter Folliss, also moved on to the Secret Intelligence Service. Ralph Vibert was another of the Beaulieu staff who eventually became a Chief Instructor at a similar school in the Far East, in the autumn of 1943. After the war he returned to Jersey as an advocate, became the Solicitor-General and a prominent Jersey politician.

The Beaulieu team seem to have turned to Scotland Yard for assistance in designing the module on criminal skills. Two sources of evidence indicate that they produced a professional burglar and safebreaker to teach the Beaulieu students how to blow the locks off safes and doors. During the war Woolrych mentioned to one of his sons, a regular naval officer, that he had a professional burglar on his staff but did not reveal his name. In May, 1941, lockpicking, keymaking, housebreaking and safe-blowing were being taught by Captain D.E.F. Green, always known as 'Killer' Green, of the Intelligence Corps. Everybody, including many of his colleagues, were convinced that Green had been 'inside', because of his adroitness at breaking into houses, picking locks and breaking into safes. It is most unlikely that he would have been awarded the King's Commission had he been a convicted criminal. He was by profession a Chartered Accountant who is said to have learned his nefarious skills from an incorrigible Scottish burglar and safebreaker, Johnny Ramenski, who was of Polish extraction and was destined to spend thirty-eight years of his life in gaol.

Ramenski is said to have been the first Beaulieu instructor in criminal skills. He had been released from Barlinnie gaol in Glasgow for war service, probably in exchange for a reduction in his sentence. He was not recruited into the army but remained a civilian instructor, though when teaching he wore army overalls, thus giving rise to the rumour that he had been conscripted. He was about twenty-seven years of age, five feet ten inches in height, heavily built, had a swarthy, unwashed and severely pock-marked complexion and spoke with a thick Glagwegian accent. His services were employed by the army in several establishments to teach troops safe-blowing and he is reputed to have been used by the Foreign Office to blow open a Foreign Embassy safe on at least one occasion. Early in February, 1942, he is known to have been instructing commandos at the Combined Operations Depot at Achnacarry, fourteen miles to the north-east of Fort William, and moved from there to teach the use of explosives to the Royal Engineers at their depot at Ripon.

He was a dab hand with explosives and detonators but was very difficult to understand, so thick was his accent, and if interrupted during a demonstration would growl 'hush yer greetin'. He had an extraordinary knack of knowing just how much explosive to use on a job and he was also a fine judge of how to make the force of the blast go into the lock leaving a neat hole and not exploding outwards to wreck the room. He had various tricks for containing the blast to the lock, like packing mud round the explosive or using a long piece of timber as a brace between the explosive and the wall of a room. He also taught his students how to deaden the noise of the explosion.

Ramenski is said to have spent some time teaching at Beaulieu, before his subject was taken over by 'Killer' Green and later by Scotland Yard professionals of the Burglary Squad. Since he was a civilian he could not be housed in army barracks and where he lived, whether in lodgings under police supervision or in a local prison, is not known. What is known is that his 'war service' was interspersed with stretches in prison for further offences. He was a compulsive burglar and safe-breaker.

Almost every book written by former agents about their time at Beaulieu mentions Captain William Clark, always known as 'Nobby', who, throughout the war, taught living off the land and fieldcraft, how to move stealthily through woodland and open country. He had been a regular soldier, a veteran of the First World War, with twenty-two years service in the army and had risen through the ranks. He was a big, burly man with hands like hams and had a shock of black hair and a complexion 'like a glass of claret'. Usually he had a pair of labradors at his heels. He had been a gamekeeper on the Royal Estate at Sandringham and was probably the only member of the Beaulieu instructor staff who was not fluent in a foreign language, although he could speak a little soldier's French. At Beaulieu he was both a 'housemaster', the adjutant of STS 35, The Vineyards, and the best known instructor on the Survival module which included lessons in poaching. During the threatening days of a German invasion he also instructed staff and students in the use of firearms and explosives in isolated quarries and clay-pits in the vicinity of the Beaulieu estate. He had been a key member of the party designated to stay behind at Beaulieu and in the New Forest in the event of invasion.

He was also the source of continuous irritation to the Montagu Land

Agent, Captain Widnell, who thought that there was nothing so deadly as a gamekeeper turned poacher. Clark was frequently accused of overstepping his authority in the liberal use he made, without Widnell's permission, of the facilities, the woodland and the game on the Montagu estate. He tried Widnell's patience to the limit and caused the latter to write repeatedly to the School's commandant, complaining of Clark's misdemeanours, like devasting a copse of saplings to provide wood for a hide.

There is no doubt at all of 'Nobby' Clark's remarkable skills as a stalker, trapper, poacher of game and fish and his ability to conceal his movements and himself, despite his bulk, in any type of country. He was an expert at laying traps, primitive but very effective alarms and security devices to protect property and ensnare trespassers and undesirables. After all, it had been one of his duties at Sandringham to protect royal personages.

He was not the only member of the staff to teach living off the land. Several other officers including Captain Maurice Bruce were engaged in the same task at various stages of the war but one unexpected instructor, at STS 34, The Drokes, in its early days, was another former gamekeeper, Private Len Hatfield, whose talents were also used to teach many student agents poaching and trapping and how to live rough, before he was posted to active service.

Although many of the Beaulieu staff were originally specialists in particular subjects they do not appear to have remained so for very long. For example, it is known that Paul Dehn also taught codes and secret inks, and all the Intelligence Corps instructors were required to do a spell of teaching students to identify German uniforms and units, especially the military and political police and counter-espionage units and organizations such as the Gestapo, the SD, the Abwehr and similar civil and para-military organizations in all the Nazi-occupied territories. One of the earliest instructors to be given this task for a brief period was Hardy Amies, the famous couturier, who is remembered by his contemporaries for his immaculately tailored uniforms.

He had joined up at the age of 30 at the outbreak of the war and as a linguist had been posted into Field Security and later commissioned in the Intelligence Corps and posted as an Intelligence Officer to the Canadian Corps Headquarters in England. He had been interviewed and recruited into SOE in April, 1941. He was sent down to Brockenhurst station where he was met by an army driver and taken to The House in the Woods. There, he was greeted by 'a pleasant hunchback in civilian clothes, an expert in secret inks and codes', who was 'the only inhabitant of the house at that hour'. The only civilian other than Philby known to be at Beaulieu at this period was the elusive Professor Patterson, seconded from the Secret Intelligence Service.

In November, 1941, Hardy Amies was posted back to London into the Belgian Section of SOE. He eventually did the parachute course at Ringway and at the end of 1943 he became the head of the Belgium Section.

Within one year of the School's inception no fewer than eleven of the original staff had moved on and had been replaced by other instructors and 'housemasters'. Of the original instructors only five, John Wedgwood, Peter Folliss, Marryat Dobie, Bobby Angelo and Ralph Vibert, remained at Beaulieu for more than two years. Of these, Marryat Dobie was by far the oldest, indeed he was the oldest of all the instructors. He was fifty-three years of age and was a veteran of the First World War in which he had served in the original Intelligence Corps. Between the wars he was a prominent librarian and scholar and had been the Keeper of Manuscripts in the National Library of Edinburgh.

One of the original team was Henry Threlfall, an imperturbable individual who was particularly adept at getting senior staff officers to meet the needs of SOE. He came to Beaulieu after operational experience in Sweden where he had been working with the German Section. He left Beaulieu during 1942 and was posted into the operations section of the Polish Section and moved with them to their advanced headquarters at Monopoli near Bari in Italy in the autumn of 1942. It was from here in the summer of 1944 that the Poles sent their agents, many of them trained at Beaulieu, to support the Warsaw uprising. He became the head of Force 139, which was conducting operations with the Polish and Czech Sections. After the war he became the head of the Siemens organization in London.

Of the original 'housemasters' there were two who appear to have remained at Beaulieu for the entire period of the School's existence, 'Nobby' Clark and Captain R. Carr. Carr was for a long period the adjutant of The Drokes (STS 34).

Chapter VII

THE STUDENTS

The popular idea of a spy is somebody similar to Kim Philby, a civilian who may or may not be a native of the country in which he resides, posing as a respectable citizen while collecting and transmitting classified information to a foreign power. This classic notion is in fact far more descriptive of the type of people operated by our Secret Intelligence Service than the men and women who worked for SOE, whose primary purpose was subversion and disruption. Inevitably, in order to do this SOE needed a great deal of information for targeting and sabotaging installations and key industrial plants working for the Germans in the occupied countries. Some of this came from their own resources but much of it came from other Intelligence sources including air reconnaissance and the Secret Intelligence Service. Nevertheless, the Country Sections needed huge amounts of information about local regulations, documentation and living conditions in the occupied countries in order to operate at all. In practice, therefore, the SOE agents were compelled to collect intelligence for operational reasons, but it was not their primary function.

Anybody who has read some of the 400 books that have been written about SOE operations, or have read some of the personal accounts of their experiences by numerous former agents, might be forgiven if they became confused as to whether the typical SOE agent was a 'civilian' like the well-known agents of the French Section or whether they were more like the SAS men of the present day. Certainly the focus of public attention has been upon the French Section's civilian 'star' agents like Peter Churchill, John Farmer, Francis Cammaerts, Ben Cowburn and Robert Heslop. Even greater publicity has been given to the Section's fifty-five women agents, among them Odette Hallowes, Pearl Witherington, Nancy Fiocca and Christine Granville, all of whom survived, and to the eleven brave women who were caught by the Germans and perished after terrible suffering in Nazi concentration camps, women like Violette Szabo, Yvonne Rudellat and Noor Inayat Khan.

Very few people will have heard of the 'star' agents of the other Country

Sections, such as Knut Haukeld, Joachim Ronneberg, or Jens Paulsson of the Norwegian Section, or of Jan Piwnik and many other very brave Poles; or of the Dutchmen Lieutenant Jan Ubbink and Sergeant Pieter Dourlein who suffered almost as much at the hands of the British, who thought they were double agents after they escaped from the Gestapo, as they did under the Germans. And there were others, too numerous to mention, who served with distinction in the Czech, Belgian and Danish resistance movements. There is a tendency to overlook the large number of British officers and men who fought with partisans in France, Greece, Albania, Yugoslavia and other Balkan countries and never tried to disguise their true identities or their British nationality. There were also some who lost their lives operating in neutral countries in Europe, the Middle East, the Far East and elsewhere.

At a very modest estimate there were 1,200 agents working for various SOE Country Sections in France alone and the total number running around Europe has been estimated by one source as 5,000 and by another at 6,000. Probably half of them worked behind enemy lines in uniform, either of our own or of allied armies. Many of these men belonged to SAS-type units, as, for example, the Free French Savanna and Josephine parties. Some were 'in and out' parties like the commandos of the Norwegian Linge Company who provided the 'Grouse' and 'Gunnerside' teams that blew up the Norske Hydro heavy water manufacturing plant at Vemork and later sank the ferry carrying the entire German supply of heavy water in Tinnsjo. Others were quite literally commandos on raiding missions like the members of the Small Scale Raiding Force.

There was a long-running argument within the upper echelons of SOE as to whether it was better to train servicemen or civilians as secret agents, given that their purpose was sabotage and disruption. In a previous chapter it has been recorded that Bill Brooker, the man whom Philby described as the cleverest man he had ever met, was at loggerheads with Colin Gubbins over this issue and it led to Brooker's downfall. The evidence indicates that there was continual vacillation between the two types at various stages of the war, reflecting an ambivalence about the agents' roles that stained the training syllabus. The choice really depended upon numerous geopolitical factors and the precise task which particular agents were required to perform. Some, for instance, were political emissaries like Jean Moulin in France or the SAS-trained Fitzroy Maclean, Churchill's emissary in Yugoslavia. Some were resistance organizers like F. Yeo-Thomas, Peter Churchill and Francis Cammaert, or couriers, a task for which women were particularly suitable, or radio operators, or weapons and explosive experts, or local co-ordinators with Allied military operations like the Jedburgh teams. Some were servicing a network by providing premises or letter boxes or some other supporting role.

Strangely, very little has been written by or about the most vulnerable of all the secret agents, the radio operators, men and women of many nationalities who were often very young NCOs and who were usually caught by the Gestapo and the Abwehr faster than they could be trained. One expert estimated that more resistance networks were broken up through the capture of radio operators than were destroyed by penetration agents.

The radio sets they used weighed 30 lbs and could not be disguised as anything else. They could be dismantled into four parts each of which was obviously a piece of radio equipment. There were instances when operators were able to convince some inexperienced Germans that they were not radios but recording equipment. These sets could not produce more than a weak signal of 20 watts and needed an aerial 70 ft in length. They needed at least two delicate crystals, one for day and one for night operations and different ones for different transmitting frequencies. In the early days of the war the operator spent several hours a day working the set at the same time of day and in consequence all of them were caught. The Germans, who were better than the British at radio-location, could arrive on the operator's doorstep within half an hour of the start of a transmission.

The first radio operators were all men, usually selected from our own or from one of the Allied armies and had already received their basic training in morse code from their own people. They received their training in clandestine operating techniques and coding from the Royal Corps of Signals at Thame Park, and afterwards were sent to various towns in Britain for practical exercises in working a clandestine radio. They were billeted on trusted civilian families, previously vetted by MI 5, and chosen not just for their discretion but for the location of their houses and for having a tree close to an upstairs back bedroom window, from which to hang the 70ft aerial. The operators were given brief training in dodging our own radio-location experts who could locate an unidentified transmission in a matter of minutes and could converge on the locality in less than an hour, (compared with the Germans' thirty minutes). It was not until the autumn of 1941, after a number of them had been lost, that SOE headquarters woke up to the fact that the radio operators were a danger to the organizations in the field. From then on they were given security training at STS 52 at Grendon in Buckinghamshire, but it proved un-

78

satisfactory and in the spring of 1942 it was decided to send them for more thorough security training for 14 days at Beaulieu and they were housed mainly in The Vineyards (STS 35), although some are known to have been housed in The House on the Shore (STS 33).

One of the Beaulieu instructors said he thought that the first batch of radio operators, probably Dutch, to take the security course was housed in Hartford House, the smallest house in the complex, which suggests that there were only two or three of them. Philby mentioned two Dutch radio operators among the earliest students and said that they fell into German hands and were executed.

To keep the wireless operators proficient in transmitting and receiving morse code, it was necessary for them to exercise their W/T skills daily. As anyone who has learned morse code will know, speed can only be achieved when one ceases to 'read' individual dots and dashes and the groups of dots and dashes that make up the individual letters. With practice, the individual letters and even groups of letters become subliminal but this facility is very quickly lost if not constantly practised.

The radio operators of different nationalities were at one time mixed together for training in the clandestine subjects. A former Belgian agent radio operator, Jaques Doneux, in an unpublished book of his experiences, wrote that 'at Beaulieu I found I was one of eight students and this time we were a really mixed bag. There was a Belgian major, a British captain, two British lieutenants, a French lieutenant, a French pilot officer, a Polish woman who wore WAAF uniform and two British sergeants.' The language problems that this arrangement presented to the instructors can well be imagined.

A large number of operators had been lost through following a strict transmission routine at a regular time of the day and consequently later trainees were taught to move house frequently and were warned that if they valued their lives they should be brief and never transmit twice from the same place, or at the same time of day or on the same frequency two days running. Later in the war they were provided with a gadget to speed up the transmissions.

Unfortunately, even after security training, a high proportion of the radio operators remained careless and became a danger to their circuits, so much so that circuit organizers were told never to meet them. The result was that the operators were driven into social isolation, became bored to distraction and were driven to seeking indiscriminate company, usually with fatal results. However, many survived their tours of duty, and some survived several tours, like the inimitable Denis Rake of the French

Section, the gun-shy and unashamed homosexual (in the days when it was a criminal offence), who survived fantastic adventures and who during one mission lived with a German officer of like persuasion. Between missions Rake did a stint at Beaulieu as an instructor and Conducting Officer.

Some sections, particularly the Poles and the Czechs, who at an early date had built up Home Armies, drew the bulk of their agents from their own people already living in the occupied countries. Presumably these people were already vastly experienced in the day-to-day problems of living and staying alive under the Nazi régime, easily took to clandestine life because it was already part of their existence and therefore stood a better chance of survival.

It is doubtful if, after the war, a proper statistical survey and analysis was made, country by country, of which of the various sources of agents gave the best chances of survival, the SAS type of operative, the commandos, civilians recruited from outside the Nazi orbit and parachuted in or civilians trained in situ for their clandestine roles. Much depended upon the grip which the agent's circuit or the partisans exercised over their native territories, how rash or cautious they were and the very nature of the terrain over which they operated. In a small, flat, densely populated country like Holland there was nowhere for partisans to hide, whereas in Greece and the Balkan countries there were mountain fastnesses that could be strongly defended, where large groups of partisans could be supplied by air at night and could hide from German troops and aircraft by day. Similarly the arctic wastes of Norway provided large areas in which commandos could hide, providing they were tough enough to withstand the cold weather and were knowledgeable in matters of arctic survival.

There was no one type of background that fitted the agents to operate in all countries. Some were primarily soldiers, including a large number of British soldiers, some were civilian expatriates recruited from anywhere in the free world, providing they spoke the appropriate language fluently, and a substantial number of people, soldiers and civilians, were trained in situ or were brought out of occupied Europe to Britain or North Africa to be specially trained. To cope with such a wide variety of roles the Beaulieu school provided individual tuition or group tuition as required.

The traffic of people into and out of Nazi-occupied Europe during wartime was breathtakingly large and ran into many thousands if one includes all sorts of service and civilian personnel brought out by land, sea and air. In France alone 433 people were secretly evacuated by air using Lysander, Hudson and Dakota aircraft of the Special Duty Squadrons landing behind enemy lines. And 258 agents were ferried in by aircraft. The number of agents dropped by parachute is not recorded but must total thousands. Nor is it known how many agents were evacuated by overland routes. Because of incessant problems with the acquisition of aircraft and operating them at maximum range, the Czechs and the Poles were compelled to send their couriers by long and dangerous overland routes through France and Germany or Austria to keep in regular touch with events in their home countries. The principal routes into Norway were by sea, using a disguised fishing boat, the Shetland Bus, and motor torpedo boats.

Much publicity has been given to the proportion of agents who were caught and killed by the enemy, but their losses were not as great as that suffered by men serving in Bomber Command, where only 10% survived a tour of duty, or men in the D-Day assault forces where casualty rates for some units reached 95%. Indeed those serving behind the lines were a lot safer than the poor devils facing an artillery barrage and minefields on any of the battlefronts. SOE expected a 50% loss of its agents, but its true figure was about 30%, although this varied greatly according to theatres of operations and the stage of the war in which they were committed to operations. The Dutch and the Poles suffered enormous percentage losses of agents. But on balance, for SOE as a whole, more survived than died. A survival rate of 60 or 70 per cent is a tribute not only to their own ingenuity but also to their survival and spycraft training. Although the actual damage they inflicted directly by acts of sabotage was limited, there was one act which is said to have altered the outcome of the war, the destruction of the Germans' supply of heavy water, putting an end to their atomic research programme. The modest achievements of other direct acts of sabotage must be set against the agents' success in stirring up resistance among the native populations on a scale that is mind-boggling, to be counted in tens of thousands rather than in a few thousand in each country. And the extent to which the Germans' war production was crippled by an enormous number of acts of unattributable sabotage can never be measured, but it must have been colossal. Resistance ultimately made it impossible for the Germans to move about outside the main centres of population except in armoured convoys. Life for the ordinary German soldier in any occupied town was made unsafe and miserable.

The evidence of this research indicates that the first batches of agents of the French and RF Sections, and the Polish, Scandinavian, Czech,

Dutch and possibly other Sections were drawn from those nations' commandos. They were trained soldiers posing as civilians during operations and not vice versa. In 1942–3 there was a tendency to favour civilians in France, Belgium and Holland, but it seems to have been reversed as D-Day approached, with the parachuting into France behind enemy lines of SAS and at least ninety three-man Jedburgh teams.

There is no reliable record of the nationality of the first students to attend a course at Beaulieu, but in his memoirs Philby mentions that soon after the school opened and before the arrival of the 'professional' group of instructors from the Intelligence Training Centre, somebody in SOE had sent an unknown number of anti-fascist Italians to Beaulieu for agent training. Denis Hendy is emphatic that the first students billeted at The Drokes were Spaniards.

The Italians had been recruited from among Italian prisoners of war imprisoned by the British in India. Whether they were military or civilian is not known. Philby says they had been recruited by Alberto Tarchian and that they had been put in the charge of a British officer who spoke perfect Italian but who barked at them. It is believed they were accommodated at STS 35, The Vineyards. There is no record of whether any of these men were ever given any agent training, or what sort of training this might have been. And there is no record of how long they stayed or where they were sent, but it is probable that they were treated in the same way as the Spaniards.

There were twenty-five Spaniards, thirteen of them accommodated in The House on the Shore and the remainder in The Drokes. At The House on the Shore their interpreters were three young men of Field Security, Corporal Geoff Holland, and Lance Corporals Dicky Warden and Bernard Ettenfield. Peter Kemp, a well known SOE operative who re-trained at Beaulieu in the spring of 1944, before going to Russia, described the Spaniards as a villainous crowd of assassins, who after being mucked about for years by the British government would cheerfully have killed anyone in British uniform. Bernard Ettenfield, who got to know them well, recalled that they had been selected from soldiers of the Spanish Republican Army who had fled to France when defeated in the Civil War. They had joined the French Foreign Legion and when France capitulated in the spring of 1940 they had evidently managed to escape captivity and had made their way to Britain where they were enlisted into the Pioneer Corps. They were deposited at Beaulieu in about February, 1941, at a time when Hitler was attempting to drag Spain into the war. Our Intelligence services had discovered that the Chief of the Abwehr, Admiral Canaris,

16. Lieutenant-Colonel 'Bill' Brooker, a Chief Instructor, described by Philby as the cleverest man he had ever met. (*R. M. Brooker.*)

17. Cuthbert Skilbeck, a Chief Instructor, who, with Brooker, was the architect of the Security Module. (*Hamish Pelham-Burn.*)

18. Major John Wedgwood of the pottery family who was Chief Instructor for more than two years. (*Intelligence Corps Museum*)

19. Major Peter Folliss, originally Disguises Instructor, who later became the last Chief Instructor. *(Intelligence Corps Museum)*

20. Paul Dehn, Propoganda Warfare Instructor. *(Hamish Pelham-Burn)*.

21. Ralph Vibert, the Principal Instructor in Codes and Secret Inks. *(Intelligence Corps Museum)*

. The School Staff taken about November, 1941. *Standing l to r: R.* Carr (Housemaster), D. Benn, M. Dobie, G. Morton, M. Bruce, R. Angelo, P. Dehn, P. Folliss, A. Enthoven, H. Burgess. *Seated l to r:* H. Threlfall, J. Wedgwood, C. Skilbeck, (Chief Instructor), Lieutenant-Colonel Woolrych, (Commandant), Major Palmer (Adjutant), Capt Parsons (Admin Officer). *(Courtesy Mrs. Ann Sarell)*

. Alan Wilkinson, who followed Palmer as Adjutant of the School. *(Intelligence Corps Museum)*

24. Bobby Angelo, one of the longest-serving members of the School.

25. Sir Alan Campbell, another long-serving Instructor.

26. Marryat Dobie, the oldest and probably the longest-serving Instructor; he served in the Intelligence Corps during the First World War.

27. 'Pip' Whittaker, Codes and Cyphers expert. *(All Intelligence Corps Museum*

28. Dorothy Wickens, the Commandant's Secretary.

29. Phil Spriddell *(below, left)*, Secretary.

30. Ann Keenlyside *(below)*, Secretary, who also participated in Field Schemes.

(All courtesy Mrs Ann Sarell.)

31. 'Nobby' Clark, nearest camera, with other gamekeepers at the funeral of King George

32. Private Jock Flockhart, the Commandant's driver, with the Hudson Terraplane motor
(*Intelligence Corps Museum.*)

33. Members of the staff in 1942: *l to r:* Polish Interpreter, Alan Wilkinson (Adjutant), D. "Killer" Green, (Criminal Skills Instructor), Captains Hornsby and Campbell, Captain Carroll (U.S. Army), Captain R. Walters, Captain Lofts (Admin. Officer). *(Intelligence Corps Museum)*

34 Staff in June, 1944: *Back row, l to r:* Captains Delves, A. Drake, F. Rhodes, Hornsby, M. Dobie, T. Howard, A. Hinde. *Front row l to r,*

was in Spain in January, 1941, trying to get Franco to allow German troops to pass through the country to attack Gibraltar. While Franco vacillated, SOE was preparing for action in Spain. Hence its interest in the Republican cut-throats. Hitler's overtures lasted for many months and the threat of Spain joining the war as an ally of Germany remained a distinct possibility until the Germans began their invasion of Russia in June, 1941.

Bernard Ettenfield stated that the training the Spaniards received was intended to keep them busy and out of mischief; they did not receive any training in spycrafts or for specific missions behind enemy lines. Denis Hendy stated that they remained at The Drokes, (and presumably also at The House on the Shore), for at least three months, which is far longer than any of the later students who were being trained as secret agents. He confirmed that the Spaniards were kept busy with some sort of commando training, especially physical training and weapons training, and in their off-duty hours they seem to have spent much of their time playing football with the Durey boys, Denis aged 12 and his younger half-brother aged 6. They used to frighten Mrs Durey by upending the smaller boy, suspending him over a water butt and generally being over-boisterous with the boy. According to Hendy, one of the Spaniards, named Pollanca, had the most appalling scars down one side of his body from injuries sustained when a hand grenade exploded near him during the Civil War.

When the professional instructors arrived at Beaulieu in April, 1941, they were appalled at the prospect of teaching the Spaniards to be secret agents. Cuthbert Skilbeck, one of the senior instructors during this period, said that nobody knew what to do with them; they were frightful people and impossible material to turn into secret agents.

They were eventually sent away early in May, 1941. Some went with Geoff Holland to Manchester for a parachute course, but most of them were returned to the Pioneer Corps for normal duties with the Corps, probably as labourers. A long time afterwards, after the war, Bernard Ettenfield went into a restaurant in London and found one of them serving as a waiter.

A similar story of the unpromising material sent to SOE for agent training in the early days is related by Maurice Buckmaster. When he took over as head of the French Section in September, 1941, he inherited a recruit by the name of Nigel Low, a professional gambler and confidence trickster passed on to SOE by Scotland Yard, who failed to inform them of Low's criminal record and his long list of convictions. Low was a fluent French speaker and was sent to Wanborough Manor for much of his agent training. He passed all the tests with credit and was sent to France by torpedo boat in the spring of 1942, carrying a large sum of money in old French banknotes. He made his way to the Riviera and was never seen again. As far as is known he was never caught by the Germans nor by the Vichy authorities. After that episode the French Section made sure that they took careful account of recruits' gambling and drinking habits.

In his memoirs Kim Philby mentions that among the earliest students were two Frenchmen, one politically left-wing, the other right-wing, whom he trained as propagandists. One of these two students was Yvon Morandat, a young Christian trade unionist who was to carry out important missions for General de Gaulle in France.

In May, 1941, a party of twenty Norwegian soldiers, one officer and nineteen privates of the Linge Company, all in their early twenties, were billeted at The Drokes, replacing the Spaniards. Among the men was Joachim Ronneburg who was to lead the team that became famous for sabotaging the German's heavy water installations and supplies. As privates they were 'Other Ranks' and lived within the house in quarters separate from their officer, who messed with the 'Housemaster', Captain R. Carr. They were debarred from the dinner parties held in the officers' mess. They were not given batmen like many of the later student agents, but had to make their own beds and clean their own quarters.

Ronneberg who was very tall, slim and like all the Norwegians physically exceedingly tough, wrote, 'The main entrance of The Drokes was on the north side of the house. When you went inside you entered a roomy hall. A staircase on the left took you up to the bedrooms on the first floor, some faced north and some faced south looking out across the Solent to the Isle of Wight. The lecture room and the sitting room had entrances from the hall. The sitting room was in the south-west corner of the house and a door opened from it on to a veranda and a terrace that stretched along the south side of the house. A lawn led down from the terrace and was framed by a hedge overlooking the sea. To the south-west of the lawn was a little rectangular swimming pool sheltered by hedges on three sides. On the far short side of the pool was a diving board.' He failed to mention that the swimming pool was not like a modern heated pool; it was fed from a natural spring and was exceedingly cold, relying on the sun to warm the water. One of the lunchtime activities of the Norwegian soldiers was to compete with each other diving into the pool to retrieve half-crowns which had been thrown in for the purpose.

At this stage of the war the raid on the Norsk Hydro had not been envisaged and the men were undergoing basic training primarily as uniformed agents, on the offchance that they might be of some future use for work in enemy-occupied Norway. They were given only limited training in the spy crafts but received a fairly rigorous training in security. Afterwards they were posted to Scotland for general mountain warfare training and it was to be a long time before any of them saw active service in Norway.

Although the Norwegians were forbidden to go outside the grounds of the estate they did so nonetheless on a number of occasions, dressed in battledress trousers and civilian pullovers, posing as civilians. One day a party of them wandered out of the grounds during the morning and found their way to the Turfcutter's Arms at East Boldre where the locals treated them to endless drinks. They tumbled out of the pub at closing time and were staggering back towards Beaulieu when a car load of Field Security men brandishing small arms fell upon them and arrested them as German agents. They were taken back to The Drokes and then sent up to London, to the Norwegian Section headquarters to be severely reprimanded.

A substantial proportion of the 400 Norwegian agents were trained at Beaulieu and are known to have been housed in Hartford House, The Vineyards, Boarmans, Warren House and Clobb Gorse, as well as at The Drokes.

On the other side of the Beaulieu River, at Boarmans, the first women agents of the French Section had arrived. There were four of them, Yvonne Rudellat, Andrée Borrel, Marie-Therèse le Chene and Blanche Charlet, accompanied by their conducting officer, Pru Macfie of the FANYs. It is said that the arrival of women for training as secret agents caused much consternation and some horror among many of the Beaulieu tutors. Two of these women, Yvonne Rudellat, a Canadian, and Andrée Borrel who was French, were caught by the Nazis and died in concentration camps.

The first group of Polish students did not arrive at Beaulieu until early in 1942. Before this date resistance in Poland had been carried out by disparate groups fighting both the Soviet Russians and the Germans. In 1942 they were formed into the underground Home Army. On 11 April a group of Polish students, probably the very first group, fifteen of them under a conducting officer, Captain Zelkowski, arrived at Beaulieu and were accommodated in The Drokes and thereafter the Poles seem to have arrived regularly in batches of fifteen or more and were accommodated in The Drokes and The House on the Shore. There is documentary evidence that they took the Beaulieu course in May and July, 1942; in June, 1943, they sent a senior air force officer with one course of fifteen students to appraise the syllabus and he suggested some modifications. In March, 1943, the Polish secret service occupied Inchmery House while continuing to send students to Beaulieu. The last course for the Poles ended on 22 September, 1944, while the Warsaw uprising was in its dying phase. It is not known how many of the Poles who did the course at Beaulieu were among the 318 men parachuted into Poland to help the Home Army during the course of the war. Nor whether the last course finished their training before Poland was liberated.

Among the many Poles trained at Beaulieu was Jan Piwnik, known as Ponury (Grim), which aptly described his habitual expression, famous for his daring raid on Pinsk prison (now in Belorussia) to release members of the Resistance. With equal daring he also dressed himself in a German SS uniform, held up a German troop train, walked through the train ordering the Germans to hand over their weapons which he then passed out of the windows to awaiting partisans! He was killed in a partisan battle with the Germans at Jewlasze on 16 June, 1944.

The glamour of espionage and other forms of resistance activity tends to overshadow the bread and butter work of the Beaulieu organization. Although many kinds of secret agents were trained there, a significant proportion of the trainees were being prepared for other, very varied overt and covert activities, and it is possible that half the trainees were never dropped behind enemy lines and never went anywhere near the battlefield. A large number of the Beaulieu students were British and foreign officials of the Country Sections or were on the SOE headquarters staff. One of there was Vera Atkins, the Chief Intelligence Officer of the French Section and a powerful figure within SOE, who paid several visits to monitor the courses, sat in on the Security lectures and admits to participating in a burglary exercise, sneaking about in the forest like a footpad in the dead of night, acting as the lookout for a raiding team.

Some of the students were being trained as trainers for SOE schools in other parts of the world or as liaison staff to work with Allied countries such as Russia and America. Several parties of Americans were trained at Beaulieu which at one stage had on its training staff an American officer, Captain Carroll.

Many of the Beaulieu students were posted to Commonwealth missions or to SOE missions in neutral countries all over the world, some of which were hazardous, like the pair of Beaulieu-trained agents who were sent to Iran, a neutral country, and were subsequently murdered at the instigation of German agents. Also a substantial number of British, Commonwealth and foreign personnel including Americans, were sent to Beaulieu for what might be called 'appreciation' courses, the object of which was to 'sell' the Beaulieu training package. Special courses were run to gain the co-operation of other organizations such as various branches of the armed services, Scotland Yard and MI 5's Regional Security Liaison Officers.

The course for higher grade agents lasted three weeks. For couriers and radio operators it lasted between three weeks and ten days. For non-operational personnel it lasted between ten and fourteen days. But within these parameters the training needs for specific groups varied enormously in length and emphasis. Such a variety could be easily accommodated in the Beaulieu complex of scattered houses of varying capacity. It was not unusual for a single student agent to be coached on his or her own, and there is one documented case of a woman trainee being accommodated on her own in one of the cottages in the grounds of The Rings. Two or three trainees of the same nationality undergoing similar training could be accommodated in Hartford House whereas the much larger facilities of The Drokes and The House on the Shore could accommodate about twenty students providing they were taking the same type of course. One of the instructors, Ralph Vibert, stated that at any one time there were usually four courses running simultaneously.

For all the students being trained for operations in the field, and for those being trained as trainers or controllers of agents, the school staff, including the Conducting Officers, were required to prepare reports on their performance. One such report, on a Polish student agent, has survived. It was completed early in 1942 by one of the former Chief Instructors and is clearly a home-made and naive attempt at performance appraisal, but no worse than many in use in industry today. It is disappointingly vague and couched in subjective phrases that are nearly useless for career decision-making. It says nothing about the man's skills as an agent. Instead it reads:-

> 'A first class man of high intelligence.
> He has a good organising brain and is
> capable of thinking logically and
> thoroughly. A striking personality, both
> calm and steady with a deep sense of
> responsibility. Is capable of exercising
> authority and would inspire all with
> respect and confidence.'

It is not the kind of report on which life and death decisions on the individual's future should be made and there is little wonder that the heads of the Country Sections sometimes chose to ignore them in favour of their own assessments. Hopefully, reports compiled later in the war, when more practical forms of training had been introduced, were more informative.

Some of F Section's most famous women agents, including Odette Hallowes and Noor Inayat Khan, both of whom distinguished themselves in the field, were given adverse reports from the school which regarded them as temperamentally unsuitable for operations. Both were caught by the Gestapo and the latter paid the supreme penalty.

There must have been many who failed the course and were rejected for operations. The percentage of failures may never be known. The disposal of those who had failed and been rejected must have presented the authorities with quite a problem. They could not be returned directly to any unit outside the SOE orbit in case they talked about their spycraft training. Some sources refer to the existence of a 'Forgetting School' where failed male agents lingered interminably until they had forgotten most of what they had learned. In all probability failed agents were sent on numerous weapon and commando or special service courses to crowd their minds with more pressing information and overwhelm their Beaulieu training, before being assigned for years to a training unit or to one or other of the SOE establishments to perform some sort of teaching or administrative role. Some are known to have been sent back to SOE's commando school at Arisaig to spend a long period performing minor training functions. Others are said to have been sent to an establishment at Inverlair in the remotest part of the Scottish highlands where they were kept until all the successful agents with whom they had trained were out of harm's way, after which the failed students were returned to the general manpower pool, as had been the unwanted Spaniards in the earliest days of the School. What was done with the women trainee agents who failed is not recorded. They had been specially recruited and enlisted into the Womens' Auxiliary Air Force or the First Aid Nursing Yeomanry; the latter had plenty of jobs into which failed agents could be assigned and kept within the SOE orbit, such as domestic servants in the Holding Stations, or drivers and clerks in any one of a large number of SOE establishments.

Chapter VIII

DOCENDO DISCIMUS
(We Learn by Teaching)

The skeleton syllabus agreed by Gubbins and the SOE headquarters training staff had, according to Cuthbert Skilbeck, been fleshed out by the Beaulieu instructors. Woolrych, with his First World War experience, had undoubtedly had a hand in designing the module on Enemy Organizations and how to recognize them by their uniforms, badges and equipment. Brooker and Skilbeck designed the Security module and Folliss designed a segment of it concerned with Disguises. Professor Patterson and his successor, Ralph Vibert, had devised the module on Codes, Ciphers and Secret Inks. Philby and Paul Dehn had designed the Propaganda Warfare module. 'Killer' Green, with the help of experts from MI 5, Scotland Yard and a professional burglar had created an unforgettable module on Criminal Skills. And 'Nobby' Clark had devised his demonstrations and exercises in Survival and Living off the Land.

One subject that has not yet been mentioned because it was a commonplace feature of just about every course run by the armed services, is Physical Training and Unarmed Combat. Regular physical training was necessary in this instance to keep the trainees supple enough to maintain their skills in unarmed combat and 'silent killing' and keep them fit enough to avoid serious injury when dropped by parachute, which in those days made severe demands upon the body.

It is easy to condemn many aspects of the training programmes as amateurish. And so they were by today's standards and even by the standards of the Cold War. But allowances must be made for the urgent circumstances of the war and for the fact that there was little previous knowledge or experience of training agents for what was then a new and novel role. Moreover they were trained in an age which preceded many modern developments in fields of espionage and sabotage and much else that we now take for granted. For instance, wireless telegraphy transmission depended upon unreliable valve sets containing finely tuned crystals, not miniature transistors; radar, radio-location and infra-red remote control devices were in their infancy. Miniature radios, electronic transmission of signals, micro-computers and lasers had not yet been invented. Even such things as the design of parachutes and parachuting were primitive and dangerous by today's standards.

As to the urgency of those times, the whole nation teetered on the brink of a catastrophe of gigantic proportions and catastrophe did indeed overtake hundreds of thousands of families who lost their breadwinners or sons and daughters, close relatives or friends, in combat or in disasters, and many families were wiped out in the bombing of our cities.

Operational and political pressures compelled the armed services to take appalling risks and to commit men and women to combat without adequate training. The training of army units, aircrews and the crews of naval vessels was, to say the least, perfunctory and most of it had to take place on the job, with a high risk of death from inexperience. A well-known example is the rookie fighter pilots who were sent to intercept the experienced Germans in the Battle of Britain. There simply was not time to train people adequately in the face of continuous, threatening enemy initiatives on every battlefront and threatening technical developments in the performance of enemy weaponry and the invention of new devices such as flying bombs and rockets.

Expert though Beaulieu instructors may have been in their respective subjects, scarcely one of them was a former university don or professional teacher. Nearly all of them had come from businesses and the professions. Many of them had been to universities and public schools and had therefore experienced various kinds of tuition and tutorial practices. However, army personnel detailed to act as instructors received no formal training in learning theory and little tuition in instructional techniques. Teaching, like Intelligence, was regarded as merely a matter of common sense. But it is not.

From the inception of the Beaulieu school the staff encountered a number of pitfalls well known to the teaching profession concerning the programming of lecture contents, balancing a reasonable student-teacher ratio required by conventional classroom instruction against the extravagant demands of individual instruction in practical work. There were also the usual difficulties of timetabling for splinter groups scattered between numerous premises running different courses of differing duration, and the never-ending problem of updating material to keep abreast of rapidly changing events in the occupied countries.

A gnawing bone of contention among generations of schoolteachers in this country is that, although they are not allowed to teach school children until they have received lengthy, specialized training, no formal training whatever is needed to become a university don or a lecturer in higher education! The result is that the untrained and inexperienced lecturer is likely to present unstructured material that will meander over his topic because insufficient attention has been given to the thread of his arguments and to the logical arrangement and progression of his ideas and facts. Too much 'branching' from the main thrust of the lecture will leave it with all branches and no trunk, and the confused audience will wonder what the talk was all about. There is also the problem of gauging the size of the step from one concept to the next. If the steps in the sequence of the presentation are too small the speaker will be seen as talking down to his audience; if they are too large he will be accused of lofty intellectual snobbery and he will lose his audience altogether. Peppering a talk with amusing or relevant anecdotes may make the delivery more palatable, but if done by an amateur serves to divert attention from, rather than emphasize, essential issues in serious instruction.

Some lecturers attempt to avoid these hazards by writing out their lecture in full and reading it to their unfortunate students. Such a delivery does nothing to engender confidence in the lecturer's mastery of his subject and compels the serious student to spend more time scribbling than listening, thereby destroying any intelligent understanding of what is being said.

Unhappily, the tradition of education, especially higher education, in this country places far too much reliance on chalk and talk to increase the teacher-student ratio and make it look more productive. The norm is stuffing students with knowledge, often to the total exclusion of practice, or if practice is allowed it is usually insufficiently monitored or too brief to produce real skill.

When the Finishing School opened the instructor staff fell into the trap of loading the syllabuses with too much chalk and talk and not nearly enough practice and they misjudged the reactions of many of their students who were quite unlike ordinary teenage students. They varied in age between twenty and middle age, came from all walks of life and were of numerous nationalities and very varied educational backgrounds. Some, like Nancy Fiocca, already possessed years of experience operating as secret agents in enemy occupied territories. Others had suffered defeat after bitter fighting in their native countries and had experienced hair-raising adventures and hardships in order to escape to Britain. They were not hotheads by nature, nor were they criminally inclined. But their

91

commando training at Arisaig and other SOE schools, especially their training in unarmed combat, 'silent killing' and the use of close combat weapons had imbued them with supreme self-confidence. They had become doers rather than patient listeners and were not renowned for sheepish acceptance of cautionary admonitions. They were not likely to be impressed by that favourite vice of dons, the intellectualization of the trivial, nor were they likely to be overawed into acceptance of instruction by demonstrations of profundity.

It must, therefore, have been something of a shock to them to discover on their arrival at Beaulieu that they were going to have to spend much of the next two or three weeks sitting in classrooms, bending their minds to difficult subjects like codes and ciphers, the chemistry of secret inks, the complex organization of German counter-Intelligence, counter-espionage agencies and military and civil police; and above all they were impelled to absorb the cautionary practices of security, a subject that would be critical for their survival in the field but which went directly counter to their commando training.

The trainees often arrived singly or in pairs by rail at Brockenhurst or Beaulieu Road stations where they would be met by a pick-up driven by one of the soldiers from the house in which they were to be billeted. Sometimes they arrived in small groups accompanied by their Conducting Officer, a male or female official from one of the Country Sections who often also acted as their mentor and, if necessary, their interpreter and who often participated in the course as a student.

On arrival at the School some of the students had already been given a *'nom de guerre'* and a suitable new 'identity' and 'cover story' to go with it, (known to the Cold War generation as a legend) and they had to live with their new identities throughout the course. The Commandant probably knew their real names, but these were never disclosed to the instructors or to the 'housemasters' and it is said that their real names were also unknown to their fellow students. The Poles did not consider it necessary to provide all their students with a legend and neither was it necessary to provide one for the large number of students of many nationalities who were going to work with partisans or who were not going to be sent on operations behind enemy lines.

The assembling students would be greeted at their house by its 'house-master' who might or might not have a fluent command of their language, and if not the Conducting Officer would translate for him. Once they had settled into their house they received an early visit from either the Commandant or the Chief Instructor who greeted them officially and gave them a fairly lengthy description of the course content and its aims.

Complaints about the sedentary nature of the course, its theoretical emphasis and lack of realism soon filtered back to the Country Sections and the training division of SOE's headquarters in London and led some of the students who were already experienced operatives to condemn the courses as a waste of time.

A post-war report on the situation noted: 'It was found that theoretical instruction was of little value unless it could be applied in practice . . . and, furthermore, it was unsatisfactory to impose an entirely sedentary life on students who had for the past two months been living an active physical existence.' In another section of the report it mentioned that early in the School's existence it was found that 'training a man or woman to lead a clandestine life was more a question of inculcating a habit of mind than of teaching facts'. It concluded that except for students of outstanding abilities 'it was virtually impossible to teach the students all that they needed to know and also change their thinking habits in a matter of three weeks.' It does not mention the ambivalence and incompatibilities of the SOE agent's roles, the clash between the need for secrecy and the objective of creating mayhem. It was left to the Beaulieu staff to undertake the impossible task of trying to weld the two aspects together into a coherent whole.

Many of the first Beaulieu instructors were well aware of the inadequacy and amateurism of their efforts and their failure to capture the interests of the students in some of the subjects. Hardy Amies stated that before he arrived at Beaulieu he had no knowledge of enemy organizations and had to mug it up rapidly and then teach it to the students. Philby was one of the first instructors to note the indifference of most of his pupils to his sessions on political warfare. In retrospect this subject does seem to have been out of place in a programme designed for spies, saboteurs and hell-raisers. Another instructor, 'Nobby' Clark, is said to have commented on the uselessness of teaching living off the land to people who were going to become urban guerrillas or would be spending their time in the arctic wastes of Scandinavia.

The instructors learned by experience and by trial and error to adjust the ratio of theory to practice. Some subjects such as recognition of enemy units, uniforms and badges and learning a code, then encoding and decoding it, were clearly best taught in the classroom, and some, like living off the land, were clearly of a practical nature. But in between there were many topics like learning to resist interrogation, contacting strangers, identifying contacts from descriptions and the criminal skills where the balance between theory and practice was difficult to achieve and where practice presented very real problems of supervision and control and a high risk of betraying the whole secret enterprise to the public. Burglary and housebreaking, making reconnaissances of premises and breaking into potential sabotage targets such as military establishments, docks and harbours, railway sidings and other vital installations to lay specimen explosive charges exposed the students to the vigilant public alerted by constant official exhortations to watch for enemy agents and careless talk. There was not only the risk of arrest, but a very real risk of being beaten up as suspected spies by off-duty servicemen or zealous civilian vigilantes. In addition, such practical sessions introduced serious problems of monitoring and supervision and made excessive demands on the limited number of tutors trying to cope with the lecture loads and the running of courses in the other houses of the School. As it was, the practical sessions in living off the land were exposing the students and instructors to the wrath of local landowners for trespassing, poaching and damage to crops, copses, thickets and woodland in the processes of acquiring material for making hides. And small-arms fire and minor explosions were not going unnoticed in the rural community.

Indoor exercises were easy to arrange but there was a temptation to indulge in role-playing, which is patently unrealistic unless performed by people with considerable acting skill. There was only one such on the staff and that was Peter Folliss. One of the exercises was approaching a stranger and making contact without arousing the suspicions of onlookers; another was picking out an individual at an identity parade from a written or verbal description. Others were an observation exercise and interrogating trainees to try and break their 'cover' and alibis, where the interrogator was a role-playing tutor.

Initially, practical outdoor and indoor exercises were of a very modest nature. Cuthbert Skilbeck described how the Beaulieu tutors introduced one on the first course for the first batch of women trainees who were housed in Boarmans in May, 1941. The five women on this course had been driven in the dead of night a short distance from Boarmans to Hilltop and the adjacent Beaulieu Heath, several square miles of bracken, gorse, hidden ponds and bogs and generous animal and insect life. The trainees were dropped separately dressed in jump suits and parachute harnesses. Hiding in the undergrowth, they had to wriggle out of their suits and harnesses, bury them without trace, get their bearings and then crawl away from the 'dropping zone' and warily find and make contact with their 'reception committee' representative. The bogs and ponds on the

94

heath are dangerous and the women are said to have been petrified of the darkness, the desolation and the strange noises of the night life!

An early indoor exercise in observation and reporting comprised a member of the staff walking into a room for five minutes and after he had left the students were required to write a description of him. They usually made a complete mess of it until they had been taught a method of systematically assessing physical and behavioural characteristics according to a schedule.

Bearing in mind that several batches of students of different nationalities might be undergoing training simultaneously on different types of courses of different lengths, the problem of resourcing and timetabling the course for each house must, as already mentioned, have been a nightmare. Cuthbert Skilbeck said that he and Bill Brooker used to reserve Sunday mornings for this onerous task, using an enormous blackboard which covered one wall of their office in The Rings. They had to arrange their complex training schedules by trial and error. It was an extremely difficult task that sometimes spilt over into the afternoon. They had sixteen instructors, many of them specialists in particular subjects, nine student houses, six or seven different subject modules and about eight teaching periods during the day, as well as one or more at night, and they had to allow sufficient time for the tutors to move by road from one house to another varying in distance between two and ten miles. Shuffling all these variables without the aid of a computer to produce a workable timetable must have been a challenge to the sharpest of intellects.

One of the outcomes was that the specialists did not remain as specialists for very long and in order to meet the demands had to turn their hands to teaching some of the more general matters like German organizations and resistance to interrogation. Ralph Vibert, the original coding expert, also participated in field exercises and acted as an interrogator (he had been a barrister) in training the students to rehearse their cover stories and resist interrogation. Paul Dehn, the propaganda expert, is also known to have taught codes, ciphers and secret inks. As the practical exercises grew in length and complexity the 'housemasters', the other ranks who worked in the houses, the Field Security staff attached to the School and even the three secretaries were drawn into the training programme in a variety of instructional, observational and participant roles.

Because of the different types of work for which the students were being trained, the number of modules that they took, the extent to which the subjects were covered and the sequence in which they were taught varied greatly. In some cases, for example, those destined to work with partisan

95

groups to train them in the use of weapons and explosives would not need to take the module on propaganda warfare.

The instructors at the Finishing School tried exceedingly hard to keep pace with operational developments in enemy-occupied territories. They regularly received updated information from a variety of other Intelligence sources and also from enemy broadcasts and publications. They spent many hours updating their information on conditions in Nazi-occupied Europe, in Italy, the Balkans, North Africa and the Middle East, and eventually information on the Far East and Japan. The Country Sections regularly sent them information and also sent experienced secret agents down to Beaulieu, on completion of their tours of operations, to pass on their experiences and inject realism into the tuition. Such was the complexity of keeping abreast of local conditions that it was not long before the officers teaching this subject and enemy organizations were forced to specialize in a single occupied country.

Paul Dehn is reputed to have been the first instructor to introduce the idea of the complex one, two and four-day schemes during which the students were sent all over the country to major cities and ports to practise their nefarious skills and learn to cope with being shadowed, genuinely arrested, imprisoned in a police cell and interrogated for real.

The dates on which the schemes were introduced is not known, but the shorter schemes lasting one or two days were usually conducted in the nearby towns, Southampton, Portsmouth and Bournemouth. The centres of Southampton and Portsmouth were destroyed by German bombing early in the war and so most of these exercises took place in Bournemouth which was relatively unscathed. It was in the centre of the town that the trainees practised shaking off somebody shadowing them and shadowing somebody themselves, making contact with an unknown person at a prearranged spot, exchanging identification and passing messages without appearing to do so. The trainees were told never to be late or too early for a contact. One male trainee, briefed to make contact with a woman outside the Post Office, arrived a little early and approached a woman who turned out to be an innocent bystander. He apologized and circled the block again and saw another woman waiting, as he thought, to contact him, but she too was the wrong person. He circled the block again and when he approached the third woman who was his assigned contact an elderly lady beat him over the head with her umbrella and threatened to call the police and have him arrested for molesting and trying to pick up three young ladies! There is no record of what his assailant thought when he succeeded on the third occasion!

The shadowing exercises usually led the trainees into one or other of the well-known Bournemouth departmental stores, Beales, Bealsons or Plummers. There are some very amusing stories about these exercises. On one occasion the trainee proved more expert than his shadow. The trainee was Jack Trott, a married army officer, who was eventually posted to Turkey as an agent. In the spring of 1944 he was being shadowed in Bournemouth by a much younger man, probably a Field Security corporal in civvies. Trott shot into Bealsons and headed for the lingerie department where he took his time examining a selection of ladies' underwear while his highly embarrassed 'tail' hovered at the entrance until his bashfulness compelled him to retreat, allowing Trott to disappear out of another exit.

To this day the management of Beales is unaware that it took an important part in the training of many famous male and female SOE agents of many nationalities, including Odette Hallows, Violette Szabo, Andrée Borrel, Yvonne Rudellat and many others, many of whom were caught by the Gestapo.

The trainees were taught a variety of ways of shaking off a tail besides using premises like departmental stores and cinemas. They learned how to make use of reflections in shop windows to check if they were being tailed and to double back on their tracks, make last-minute boardings of public transport and taxis, alter their appearance in a doorway by donning a cap and spectacles and many other tricks.

The complex ninety-six hour schemes were introduced in the early part of 1942. The schemes involved sending groups of students to areas remote from the School to make a reconnaissance of a target area, such as a port or military establishment or railway network to determine the most vulnerable point for attack. The students were allocated individually to lodgings in widely spaced parts of the same town or in different towns, and were required to organize themselves clandestinely and carry out the orders of their group leader who had the responsibility of allocating duties and planning the attack. Whether or not the team made an actual attack using dummy explosives is not recorded.

It was discovered that too much time was wasted by the trainees keeping in contact with each other and the only person really tested was the group leader who was compelled to shoulder too much responsibility. There were also very considerable problems of supervision. A new scheme was therefore evolved in which the students were sent out individually to contact and recruit an unknown individual and perform a limited reconnaissance task. This type of scheme took a lot of planning and organizing and involved the co-operation and intervention of MI 5 agents, civilian residents, Field Security personnel and the civil police. The trainees were kept under constant surveillance and when they were caught they were arrested, imprisoned and subjected to real interrogation. There are recorded instances in which those trainees who managed to achieve their objectives and escape from the area were sent back to be arrested and interrogated, since these experiences were regarded as essential parts of their training.

Organizing these schemes became a full-time job for several members of the Beaulieu instructor staff.

Considerable opposition to this new type of scheme was encountered from some of the Country Sections who argued that exposure to arrest and interrogation was lowering the confidences of their trainees at a time when they were in a highly strung condition. But SOE's Training Division believed that it was better to discover the weaknesses of potential agents before they were sent on operations in the field where they would probably jeopardize the safety of the organization as well as the lives of their compatriots. On the whole the students reacted favourably to their ordeal and found it valuable when they were sent on real operations. This type of scheme was later adopted by the Secret Intelligence Service.

It took more than two years of constant adjustments to produce a set of courses that satisfied the needs of the Country Sections and met their approval. The length, type and content of the Beaulieu courses underwent many changes. In the earliest days specialized courses were being run by Philby exclusively for propaganda agents, in the days before this subject became the prerogative of a break-away section of SOE that became the Political Warfare Executive. Running concurrently were special time-filling courses for the Spaniards, and special agent training for Dutch W/T operators. The first consolidated courses under the Munn régime were intended only for high-grade resistance organizers and incorporated railway sabotage and reception committee training which taught agents to select suitable landing grounds for Lysander aircraft, parachuted agents and supply drops and how to arrange an appropriate number of sub-agents to collect and hide new arrivals and their supplies. It very soon became apparent that these were specialized subjects and that the Beaulieu instructors lacked the necessary expertise. These topics were made into specialized courses and were moved elsewhere.

Later still, when the principal topics of the course had been stabilized and standardized, a variety of shortened versions of the three-week course were introduced. Some of these were officially described as 'Elementary' and lasted ten days. They were intended to be 'appreciation' courses to familiarize personnel from other Intelligence agencies with SOE's activities and some were run specifically for Public Relations purposes for a variety of service and civilian units. In 1943 a two-week postgraduate course was launched, but it failed to gain the support of the Country Sections and only two such courses were run. They were intended to train students destined for particular missions in agent techniques and allowed time for revision of the trainees' weakest subjects. But time could not be afforded by the Country Sections.

Some of the successful agents and some who had worked in the Resistance before being flown back to this country for formal training said that their training was unrealistic and a waste of time, but these were in the minority. The Polish authorities and the Norwegians are known to have been mostly eloquent in their praises, with some reservations, and their nominated students were queuing up for places on the Beaulieu courses. One Polish report on the school, dated September, 1944, (the time of the Warsaw uprising) spoke of 'the very high opinion they have in the Field of the results of training at STS 33'. This was The House on the Shore.

The administrative organization of the Beaulieu training staff eventually settled into five departments. Department A dealt with Agent Techniques; B with organizing exercises; C with Enemy Organizations; D with Propaganda, and E with Codes, Ciphers and Secret Inks. However, the staff was not rigidly compartmentalized.

Chapter IX

SPYCRAFTS

During the inter-war years J.F.C. Holland, Colin Gubbins and some of the other founder-members of SOE had made a study of the organization and *modus operandi* of guerrilla and terrorist organizations all over the world, including the IRA. Also, MI 5 and the Special Branch of Scotland Yard had gained much experience of overt and covert Communist organizations and their methods of operation. In addition, Stanley Woolrych and several former Intelligence officers in SOE headquarters pooled their experiences from the First World War.

There was, therefore, a considerable body of knowledge quite separate from that possessed by the Secret Intelligence Service, which had refused to help, on various ways of arranging, controlling and operating networks of secret agents. The Beaulieu instructors were able to use this material for teaching the SOE trainees the fundamentals of sub-agent recruitment, motivation and organization and how to protect their networks by using a variety of personal and organizational security measures, including mobility and evasion.

There is an old adage which says that MI 6 recruited agents from among the aristocracy in order to penetrate the highest levels of society and provide an ear to the policy-makers and strategists, working from the top down. Whereas SOE was said to work from the bottom up, worming its way into the midden of society to spawn as much trouble as possible as widely as possible among the lowest levels of the social scale. Scurrilous though this is, there is some truth in the underlying principle. SOE did try to work from the bottom up by penetrating the work forces of essential services, the utilities, the railways, the telephone and communications networks and workers in factories. In this respect it had much in common with communist penetration.

The type of person recruited as a sub-agent and the number that made up a cell depended on the opportunity that their occupations afforded for causing disruption or for providing access to premises or important information or for gaining access to professional, occupational or trade associations, including trade unions. An important consideration was the degree to which the sub-agent could be trusted to keep secrets and exercise discretion.

The trainees were taught how to create a network of sub-agents and arrange them into independent cells with a variety of chains of command, and how to link them with alternative methods of horizontal and lateral communication, with cut-outs in the system to prevent the network being rolled up from one cell to the next by counter-espionage organizations. The cell might consist of only one person, as, for example, the key Norwegian scientist working inside the Norsk Hydro plant that produced heavy water for the Nazis' nuclear research programme. It might consist of dozens of agricultural workers and their farm vehicles organized to collect several canisters of arms parachuted into an isolated field and whisk them away to hiding places in scattered farm buildings.

The cut-outs could take various forms. Perhaps the best known is the Dead Letter Box, a cavity in a wall, a tree or a litter bin or piece of furniture or any other inconspicuous orifice, into which messages could be left for others to collect. An alternative was to use a 'post box', for example a busy chemist's shop into which messages could be dropped for later collection. Yet another cut-out was the use of a once-off 'dead' messenger, an innocent party to carry wittingly or unwittingly a message from one point to another. There are numerous variations.

The recruitment of suitable couriers to link the cells was also taught at Beaulieu. Trainees were told to seek them from among people whose occupations provided natural cover for human traffic, or whose occupations took them out and about. These included doctors, dentists, postmen, train drivers and guards, itinerant salesmen and drivers of all classes of vehicles.

The payment and remuneration of agents and helpers was also part of the curriculum for trainee resistance organizers. There was, apparently, an agreed scale of remuneration for services rendered, depending upon the motives for helping. A doctor or a railwayman might help out of patriotism, but a smuggler or a black marketeer demanded their own prices for services rendered. Others would be satisfied if their expenses were defrayed, or if they were supplied scarce or rationed goods such as food or petrol.

The selection and acquisition of premises was a vital element in agent operations. Agents and sub-agents needed to be very mobile, not just to keep in touch with their networks but for their own safety so as to avoid going habitually to one address and going regularly at particular times of the day. They needed widely scattered premises for themselves to live in,

101

places for meetings with other agents, as well as 'safe houses' in which to hide if they were being pursued, and for storing illegal equipment such as supplies of arms, radios, forging equipment or illegally acquired documents like real or forged ration cards and passes. Some of the agents who were most successful at eluding arrest never spent more than one night in the same place and some made good use of 'Nobby' Clark's survival training to sleep rough in hides built in the countryside rather than risk living in towns or villages.

All students destined for enemy-occupied territories, whether as secret agents or to work with local partisans, were given many hours of training in the recognition of enemy uniforms, equipment and the functions of a host of political, military and civil organizations which constituted a threat to their existence. The subject is far more complicated than one might expect. The enemy organizations were of two sorts. One was exclusively German, the other was indigenous and specific to the occupied country in which the agent had to operate, for instance the local police forces, including the criminal police and their informer networks, as well as the special police forces raised by the occupying Germans by recruiting criminals and Nazi sympathizers, such as the much-hated Milice in France.

At the apex of them all was the *Reichssicherheitshauptamt*, the RSHA, the Reich Security Headquarters, colloquially known as the Gestapo. The Gestapo, the Nazi Party's own security organization, was a complex tangle of organizations each with their own names, which penetrated every level of German politics and society, all spying on each other as well as upon every aspect of the military and social fabric of Germany which was riddled with informers and informer networks. It included the infamous SS that ran the concentration camps. The branch of the Gestapo that the arrested SOE agents were most likely to encounter was the *Sicherheitsdienst*, the SD, which had a pre-war strength of 100,000 detectives, agents and informers in Germany.

The Gestapo oversaw three main branches of state security and eventually seized the fourth, the Military Intelligence service, the *Abwehr*. It controlled the German secret police, the *Sipo*, and the German equivalent of our CID, the *Kripo*. The Nazis added their own iniquitous security service, Himmler's SS troops and the Sicherheitsdienst.

The Sipo (very roughly the equivalent to our Special Branch but with more distinctive political implications) and the Kripo sent units into occupied countries to control their civilian equivalent police forces. All the German services used a range of well-known methods for recruiting informers, making use of rogues and thieves, offering cash rewards for information, persecuting those who failed to inform if they were in a position to do so, blackmailing them by threatening their innocent or helpless relatives. No device was too dirty or underhanded for them to use.

The Abwehr, under Admiral Canaris, was an independent military Intelligence organisation roughly equivalent to our own military Intelligence directorates and the Intelligence Corps. After the attempt on Hitler's life in July, 1944, it was taken over by the Gestapo. It included, like our Intelligence Corps, two field organizations, the *Geheime Feldpolizei* or GFP, the secret field police akin to our own Field Security organization, and the *Feldgendarmerie*, the military police equivalent to our redcaps.

The Gestapo seized control of all the police services in the occupied countries and had to build its own networks into the social fabric of each of the newly conquered countries. The foundations had often been laid in advance of military conquest through its political organizations within such countries as Austria, Czechoslovakia, Sudetenland and even in Norway with its pro-Nazi Quisling party and in Holland where a substantial number of the native population was originally pro-Nazi.

In almost all the occupied countries the Germans formed national secret police forces out of their local sympathizers and criminals to police the native population, and these local forces were as cruel and ruthless with local 'offenders' as were their German masters. There was only one occupied country where the Germans failed to find enough local recruits to man their puppet police organizations and that was Poland.

Keeping track of all these organizations, their uniforms, equipment and their *modus operandi* required a large amount of Intelligence material from the SOE Country Sections. They were able to acquire enemy weapons and equipment and in some cases uniforms to send down to Beaulieu for Woolrych and his team to use in an updated form of instruction that was reminiscent of the system that had been used for training spies during the First World War.

There is an amusing story of how a pile of dirty German uniforms, bundled up with string and with no outer covering, was dumped out of a passing train on to the platform of Beaulieu Road station. The head porter, Percy Pearce, noted that the parcel was addressed to The Rings, which, despite all the tight security surrounding the place, he knew to be the headquarters of 'the funnies'. He phoned the School's HQ and asked them to come and collect it. He often had to phone them since a considerable number of 'lost' foreign women and men alighted by mistake from the London train at Beaulieu Road station, one stop short of Brockenhurst, their intended destination. Beaulieu Road station is situated in a desolate part of the New Forest, miles from Brockenhurst, Beaulieu and Lyndhurst. There were no names on the station platforms in those days to indicate one's whereabouts and none of the station staff called out the name of the station. The calls had ceased and the name-plates had been removed at the outbreak of the war to prevent enemy agents or invasion forces from finding their way about the country.

These uniforms were worn by members of the School's staff when subjecting the students to exercises in resistance to interrogation. They were also displayed to the students during lectures on recognition of enemy forces. But the School did not possess the complete range of enemy uniforms and unit badges and had to make do in many instances with pictures which were shown on an epidiascope, the forerunner of the modern overhead projector. Recognition exercises of uniforms and equipment, and how to identify the various units by their equipment and badges, were frequent.

The Beaulieu tutors were evidently unable to keep pace with all the changes in enemy organizations and unit badges throughout occupied Europe. In a memo to the training department of the Polish secret service, a senior Polish Air Force officer who had been sent on the Beaulieu course in the summer of 1943 wrote, 'I propose that we should eliminate from the course the teaching about the German army. Polish stations possess more detailed and recent information.'

Spies and secret agents are useless unless they can keep in touch with their controllers. There are very few means of communication; they are radio and telecommunication transmissions, written communications and visual and auditory signals. Equally, there are few modes of communication; they are radio or telecommunication signals, the spoken word and couriers, and carrier pigeons or the postal services.

Spycatchers are well aware that communications are the weakest spot of an espionage network and deploy their efforts accordingly by monitoring the air waves and telecommunication networks and making extensive use of mail interception and strict control of the movements of people. But even totalitarian régimes are unable to block all movement and communications within their homeland and conquered territories or between them and the outside world. They still need to trade with the outside world, even during periods of warfare. Iron and Bamboo curtains are a myth. They are always riddled with holes and they are often threadbare in vulnerable places. So the Nazis were compelled to allow human, postal, telephone and radio traffic within their empire and also between Germany and its conquered territories and non-belligerent nations like Spain, Portugal, Switzerland, Sweden, various African states and with South America. What they did not at first appreciate was that most of the world's telecommunication and postal traffic and much of its air traffic was routed through Britain or one or other of the British dominions and colonies! But that is another story.

The principal and preferred mode of communication for secret agents is the fastest, that is, radio transmissions or what was called Wireless Telegraphy or W/T, originally using morse code and a hand-operated key. All the students seem to have received some training in the use of morse code before they arrived at Beaulieu and many, if not all, were required to practise their skill while on the course.

A good W/T operator may be able to transmit and receive messages at about twenty-five words a minute, maybe more. But a more usual stand-ard to which non-specialist operators were trained in the armed services during the war was ten words per minute. Even short messages could be on air for several minutes, enough time for radio-locators to obtain a fix on the position of the transmissions. The Germans were particularly adept at radio-location using radio direction finding (RDF) vans and other ruses like cutting off power supplies, if necessary block by block and street by street, and watching for the transmissions suddenly to cease. Radio traffic was very vulnerable to interception and location.

Early in the war SOE struck upon the idea of sending their outgoing signals over the normal BBC overseas transmissions and no attempt was made to conceal the fact that they were signals. At a certain time of the day, or evening, an announcer would reel off, often in English, a list of meaningless phrases like 'The plum pudding is hot'. The meaning would be known only to an agent in a particular circuit in any one of the occu-pied countries, and could mean 'Cancel the operation planned for tonight.' As D-Day approached the volume of such signals increased enor-mously. Those of us who lived through the war will remember hearing these transmissions on our ordinary wireless sets between normal programmes during the evenings.

To prevent indiscriminate reading of intercepted signal traffic, senders have long made use of codes (a jumble of letters) or ciphers (a jumble of signs or numbers such as is used to call up a function on a computer). For some reason, during the early part of the Second World War, most of our intelligence services used the same system of coding, called the Playfair

105

Code, invented by Sir Charles Wheatstone. It comprised blocks of five letters or characters and could be transmitted by an expert at about two hundred characters a minute using a manual key. Some messages took twenty minutes or more to send. It took a great deal longer to encode and decode than it did to transmit. The Playfair code was soon compromised through the carelessness of operators caught by the Germans and was abandoned as too dangerous. By 1943 students were being taught the Delastelle system of coding.

The whole subject of codes and ciphers is very complex and the skill of encoding and decoding requires an aptitude for it if it is to be done with a modicum of efficiency. It is doubtful if most of the agents trained at Beaulieu had been previously tested for their aptitude for coding and so the task of learning to do it must have been a real chore for a high proportion of the students.

The same system of coding, and many variations, could be used for written messages, either written directly on to paper by secret inks, or could be picked out of passages of print in books, newspapers and magazines by pricking holes or making minute dots with secret ink over individual letters. The books or newspapers and magazines could then be sent through the ordinary post. Later in the war, in July, 1943, microphotography came into use, that is, a minute negative, the size of a printed full stop but carrying an extensive message. A microdot the size of the dot at the end of this sentence could carry many foolscap pages of typescript. The dot could be stuck on to existing print and sent through the post or by courier.

Usually the mail containing the microdot or secret message would have to pass through enemy censorship to an address in a neutral country, although some of it was undoubtedly smuggled across frontiers. The addressee was, of course, a 'post box' for intelligence traffic, and would forward the message by various means to the intended recipients.

At Beaulieu the students were taught how to make secret inks using a variety of common substances and use suitable papers, especially newsprint. The common substances included lemon and other fruit juices, urine, the white of an egg, onion juice, a sugar solution, borax, baking powder, starch, porridge fluid and blood serum. Most of these could be exposed by subjecting them to a gentle heat. The trouble with all of them was that they were Boy's Own stuff and would not pass professional scrutiny. Consequently the students were also taught how to use special chemicals that could only be exposed by subjecting them to ultra-violet light, mercury vapour, fluorescent light or ammonia fumes or other chemicals. SOE's laboratories were very ingenious not only in their research into special chemicals but also into methods of secreting them. There is a recorded instance of a pair of socks being impregnated with a secret ink chemical that could be released when soaked in water. They were carried into the field on the feet of an agent! Some of these inks were made from complex chemical solutions and required other chemical treatment to expose them.

Microphotography was taught at STS 37a, Warren House, in an isolated spot near the mouth of the Beaulieu river, from mid-1943 onwards. But there is no information available on how it was taught or by whom.

Whatever the method of coding and writing, the students were taught that if the message was being transported by a courier it should be written on a substance that was easily and inconspicuously disposable, such as cigarette packaging or sandwich wrapping, or on one that could be easily destroyed like rice paper, which could be swallowed or rolled into a cigarette and smoked. They were also taught to conceal messages in articles of clothing that could be inconspicuously discarded. They were told to avoid if possible using any of their own body orifices for concealment since if they were caught they would certainly be subjected to the indignity of a body search as a matter of routine.

The problem with using secret inks and microdots is that if they are discovered they immediately identify the sender and the receiver as secret agents or as being associated with agent networks, and invite surveillance operations to be mounted, the first step in rolling up the network.

Less incriminating were visual and auditory signals using puffs of cigarette smoke or by drumming fingers on a table top or squinting with one eye pretending to have a nervous tic or a sequence of hand or foot movements, but obviously this sort of thing had to be very brief, and had to use pre-arranged morse characters or a single sign to convey a message or expression such as 'I'm being followed' or 'I've made the drop, as arranged'.

The use of public telephones had obvious dangers but students were taught how to use negative verbal codes such as 'I had no visitors today' but meaning the exact reverse, or 'Do come by all means' meaning 'Do not come under any circumstances.' The wartime era had not got round to signalling by allowing telephones to ring a predetermined number of times or by interrupting the sequence of rings by picking up the handset and replacing it without answering.

Every student was taught how to approach a contact, known or unknown, make contact without appearing to do so and pass a message by, for example, making an innocuous comment and listening for a pre-arranged and equally innocuous reply, or by dropping a newspaper carelessly into a waste bin or upon a café table as if finished with, by sticking a message under a bench seat with chewing gum or between the slats of a seat or by throwing down an apparently empty cigarette packet or other carton.

As the war progressed the students were taught to use more complex codes and more sophisticated methods of transmission like one-time pads, microdots, and a gadget similar in appearance to an abacus, the balls of which were magnetically marked and were arranged as required in blocks of the code. Rapid transmission was achieved by wiping a stylus across the balls which sent the message at 600 characters per minute.

Almost all of the agents who were taught at Beaulieu remember their lessons in the criminal skills and many wrote about them with relish in their memoirs.

It must be remembered that in those days house building and the construction of metal safes were simpler than they are today. There were few, if any, 5-lever mortice locks and burglar alarms were unheard of. The locks on main doors were very simple rim locks screwed to the inner surface of the door and the tongue of the locks also fitted into a screw-on housing. They were therefore fairly easy to force open with a crudely made key or a piece of wire or celluloid. Almost all houses were built with ill-fitting sash windows, the glass of which had been puttied in, and most windows and french doors were fitted with paltry catches; people were more honest in those days.

Obviously the mode of entry depended very much upon whether it had to be made without leaving any evidence. If secrecy did not matter, the ubiquitous jemmy and other tools for forcing an entry, including bolt-cutters and wire cutters, would be used.

The students were taught how to break a pane of glass noiselessly by using the old Victorian burglar's method of coating a piece of brown paper with treacle, sticking it to the glass and then tapping it sharply with a hammer or even with their elbows. The paper would then be peeled off, hopefully with the shards of glass sticking to the treacle or some other sticky substance. A hand could then be put through the opening to release the catch or lock. It was also fairly easy to cut out the putty and remove the pane of glass.

Because windows and doors of many pre-war houses were so ill-fitting it was usually possible to insert a penknife or kitchen knife or a piece of celluloid into the gap that always existed where the upper and lower sashes of a window met in the middle, or between the door and the door-frame. An expert slice at the window catch, or a smart push with a piece of celluloid between the doorlock and jamb would often suffice to effect a noiseless entry.

Students were also shown stripped-down door locks to reveal their internal mechanisms and were then taught how to use piano wire to make a burglar's key to pick the lock. They were also taught how to take impressions of Yale-type and barrel keys, using soap or plasticine or modelling clay as a mould, and how to cast a new key from the mould and make skeleton keys using readily available metals such as tobacco tins. One former agent said that an outhouse at The Drokes was equipped with benches fitted with engineering vices so that the students could learn to cut and file key blanks into duplicates of the real key; it took practice to make one that worked.

Every student who attended Beaulieu seems to have a clear recollection of the safe-breaking demonstrations. At one stage of the war expertise was provided by a well-known firm of safe manufacturers on condition that they did not demonstrate how to break into their own safes! Somebody must have obtained a continuous supply of old safes for the demonstrations. 'Killer' Green, for a long time the main instructor in criminal skills, taught his pupils how to break into the backs of the safes with steel cutters, should the backs of the safe be accessible, and how to blow open the locks using a coin the size of an old penny piece, pressed into the shape of a cone and filled with half an ounce of explosive. Exactly how this was done has not been recorded! He also taught them how to blow the safe to bits, though the chances of its contents surviving intact seem dubious. The students were given some practical experience in safe-breaking by picking the locks or by making duplicate keys but for obvious reasons all of them could not practise forceful entry.

All the students were required to go on exercises in housebreaking, and every one who did remembers it as a traumatic experience. The students would be told which house to break into and would be instructed to find their way into particular rooms and break into particular desks, cupboards or filing cabinets to steal particular documents or articles to prove that they had effected an entry. The houses used most frequently for these break-ins were The Rings and The House in the Wood, and sometimes one of the student houses that was not currently in use by students, including Inchmery House, but all of them manned by members of the staff. The students, usually working in two or three-man (or woman) teams, first had to find the house from a map, make a secret reconnaissance of the property and grounds and then devise and execute the break-in and obtain proof of entry. There are numerous stories of their adventures in making the reconnaissance and the attack; men wearing women's clothing and vice-versa, so as not to arouse suspicions; hair-raising experiences creeping up gravel driveways in the dead of night trying to avoid making a noise, watching for primitive booby traps laid by Nobby Clark using thread and empty food tins containing pebbles, or trip wires; with their hearts in their mouths, breaking into premises, leaving behind a nervous lookout. And afterwards the elation of achievement with the attendant risk of an over-exuberant, careless getaway.

One English student records that after successfully 'casing the joint' by getting admission under false pretences, he made a reconnaisance inside the premises and stole a key and made an impression in a mould to make a duplicate. Subsequently, during the attempted break-in, he discovered that he had not made a very good job of making the duplicate. It failed to work and he had to get a ladder to climb into an upstairs room to gain access to the drawing room on the ground floor where he had to find and steal a vital document. Another English student reported that his team had to burgle Inchmery House during a reception that was being held there by the staff.

There is little doubt that the staff of these houses were well aware of the presence of the burglars and kept away from the rooms that were being burgled. Philby relates that on one occasion when he and other members of the staff were on night patrol round a house a whole group of Norwegians succeeded in reaching an upstairs room after penetrating thick woods strewn with alarms and booby traps laid by Nobby Clark, having crossed an open garden unseen by the patrols.

One woman agent related how she had used her safebreaking and housebreaking training to get into the Commandant's office and break open the cabinet containing her personal file in order to read the School's reports on her progress. She did not say whether she effected entry by day or by night.

Lord Montagu's mother, the Hon. Mrs Pleydell-Bouverie, who lived in Palace House throughout the war, recounted how the House was burgled at least once and the thieves, thought to have been SOE students of unknown nationality, stole a bottle of Milton from a bathroom and an unsigned cheque with the Montagu name on it as proof of entry.

In Nazi-occupied Europe strict controls were imposed upon peoples' movements and upon essential supplies, such as food, clothing, tobacco and toiletries. German administrators were notoriously bureaucratic and the native population could not survive without possessing pocketsful of permits, passes and ration cards which had to be stamped with a vast array of franks by the civil and military authorities.

SOE possessed a first-class forgery factory that could reproduce any kind of document, however sophisticated the paper, watermark, ink and typescript. Agents were provided with essential forged documents before being dropped into occupied territories, but thereafter access to professional forgeries became difficult, as was delivering them to agents in the field. Hence many students were taught at Beaulieu how to acquire by theft, burglary and false pretences, genuine documents and alter the essential details using various materials including cigarette ash to erase the critical information or dirt to fudge it and make it unreadable. They also learned how to make use of their training in inks to produce various types of ink. They learned how to make impressions of official franks and stamps and reproduce them using linoleum and other substances including the common potato. And they were taught how to forge signatures with the help of a hard-boiled egg. Exactly how the egg was used has never been revealed, perhaps to prevent the wholesale use of the technique by criminals.

Part of the forgery training involved teaching students a little about the printing trade and small printing presses. This was a subject that also formed part of their lessons in propaganda warfare so that they knew how to print mischievous pamphlets and underground newspapers.

The old *Manual of Military Intelligence*, issued shortly after the First World War, listed no fewer than thirty characteristics that should be noted by Field Security personnel when compiling descriptions of suspects. These included the obvious physical dimensions of height, weight, age and general shape, posture and gait, and mode of speech and accent or dialect. It then added a large amount of detail about the face shape, complexion, type of eyebrows, colour of eyes, shape of nose, height of forehead, hair colour and style, scars, rashes, face hair and so on.

These details provided an exceedingly useful basis for teaching the students how to disguise these dimensions of their appearances and make use of a variety of cosmetics and commonplace substances to do so. The very first lecturer in this subject was Peter Folliss, who, students and staff alike believed, had been an actor. No doubt in the occupied countries genuine stage make-up and cosmetics were difficult to obtain, but where available had obvious uses in colouring and covering or accentuating prominent facial features and blemishes and in creating blemishes where there were none. The students were also taught how to alter the shape of their facial contours by stuffing sponge pads into their cheeks, to discolour their teeth using iodine, to emphasize wrinkles using soft black lead pencils, to darken their hair with charcoal or lighten it with bleach and colouring, to blacken their jowls and make themselves look dirty with burned cork, charcoal or cigarette ash, to fake scars using collodion, a substance that forms a crinkly film or use wax to fill in chin clefts and other indentations. The use of false whiskers and wigs was also demonstrated, but if discovered during a search would obviously arouse suspicion.

It is generally well-known that recognition of familiar people at a distance takes place long before details of their faces can be seen. It is made from clues such as their mode of dress and by their characteristic gaits and other movements known to psychologists as expressive movements, or, in modern parlance, body language. Students were therefore taught the necessity of altering their mannerism, such as the way they handled and smoked cigarettes, folded a newspaper, swung their arms and the way they walked. A small stone in one shoe can produce a convincing limp and hunching one's shoulders can also make a material difference.

There are many well-known ways of altering one's appearance by altering one's characteristic style of dress, such as changing from city to country clothes, or from a tidy to a scruffy appearance, or by adding or subtracting accessories. It may sound corny, but wearing or removing a pair of spectacles, and combing one's hair on the opposite side or in a radically different way and darkening or lightening one's complexion can make substantial differences to one's appearance. Similarly, removing a raincoat or hat or putting them on can make a significant difference, especially if accompanied by a limp or hunched shoulders. Even a simple ruse such as stealing an umbrella, or disposing of one, accompanied by a change of gait can be very effective. In his autobiography Philby admits to using the raincoat, stick and hat trick to throw off the British security man following him on one particularly important occasion.

Violent criminal acts, such as sabotage, including arson, murder and assassination, were taught at Beaulieu at various stages of the war. Undisguisable acts of sabotage were classed as Attributable Sabotage in the SOE training establishments and such acts were likely to incite vengeful retaliation from the Germans. Therefore they had to be carefully considered and authorized.

In the early days railway sabotage was part of the curriculum, including sabotaging the track or the points and the rolling stock with explosives, or by manual means like prising the rails from their sleepers, loosening the gravel in the sleeper beds along a stretch of track, putting small rocks in points to prevent them being closed and damaging the axles of rolling stock. After training in the classroom, the students went to Brockenhurst station by day for demonstrations and were sent back at night to attack the main line or the sidings using dummy charges. However, it was soon realized that sabotage required specialized knowledge and special equipment, so a special course was arranged at STS 17 at Brickendonbury run by Major G.T.T. Rheam, a sabotage expert.

A spectacular derailment of an entire train is not easily organized and a railway locomotive is not easily destroyed. If it rolls off a damaged track it can be easily lifted into the upright position and placed back on the track by a crane. A small portable bomb planted on a locomotive will cause only limited damage to the metalwork. If placed against a wheel it will have no effect on the wheel's heavy steel construction, nor will it have much effect if placed against the boiler. Hiding a bomb in the coal or shovelling it directly into the furnace will cause only temporary, easily repaired damage. But, as one very successful SOE agent, Ben Cowburn, related, placing a bomb against the blocks supporting the steam cylinder will put the locomotive out of action for months. These cylinder blocks were made of cast iron and were easily cracked, and since they were parts that did not normally wear out, the workshops tended not to keep many in stock. It took quite a while to manufacture them.

However, there were some kinds of sabotage on rolling stock that could be done effectively by the inexpert and were difficult to detect. SOE parachuted into Europe a special axle 'grease' that caused the axle boxes to catch fire when the carriage was moved. It also supplied ground carborundum to put into rail-car axle boxes after the oil had been drained off. The rail-car axles then seized up.

Agents were also supplied with exploding telephones which detonated when the hand set was lifted, and exploding 'horse manure' and small 'rocks' that could be left by the roadside to be detonated under or beside enemy vehicles. Other gadgets included limpet mines that could be stuck to the sides of vehicles or ships, and bombs that could be slipped into aircraft which were exploded by air pressure when the aircraft reached an altitude of 6000 feet. A great many other devices were manufactured in SOE's workshops. Ian Fleming's fictional 'Q' in the James Bond films was directly inspired by the wartime SOE special devices workshops.

In France alone there were 144 recorded acts of industrial sabotage using a total of over 3,000 lbs of plastic explosives. Sixteen of these acts

(11%), were ineffective. A high proportion of them were against power supplies and a considerable number caused the Nazis only temporary inconvenience. As D-Day approached and on D-Day itself a large number of acts of sabotage were conducted against the railways, power supplies and telecommunication networks, causing significant disruption to the movement of German troops and supplies.

Assassination has long been an integral aspect of guerrilla warfare, but it does not appear to have been a notable feature of SOE's operations. All the agents were taught 'silent killing' using weapons or their bare hands and a few were taught to use undetectable poisons and how to dispose of corpses. Few of them were ever called upon to participate in deliberate acts of assassination, although some had the unpleasant task of executing double agents who had penetrated their networks. However, there are two well-known instances of political assassination during the war. One was the unauthorized assassination of the French Admiral Darlan in Algiers on Christmas Eve in 1942. The other was the killing of Reinhard Heydrich, 'the butcher of Prague', the top SS man in Czechoslovakia, in May, 1942. The assassins, Czech agents, were not trained at Beaulieu but at STS 17 at Brickendonbury. The assassination had been authorized by the Czech government in exile and it produced horrific retaliation from the Nazis. The assassins were caught and shot or burned alive. Ten thousand hostages were shot and every man woman and child in the village of Lidice on the outskirts of Prague was murdered, many of them burned alive in a church. The village itself was razed to the ground with flamethrowers.

The price was far too high and there were no more assassinations of high-ranking Nazis until the last week of February, 1944, by which time the Germans were being harried from every quarter in every one of the occupied countries and on such a scale that they lacked the forces to exact revenge for all such acts of resistance.

At the beginning of 1944 the Nazi security service, the SD, which was in the process of taking over the Abwehr and purging it of Admiral Canaris and his associates, was considered to be making itself such a nuisance in hazarding operations, including those in support of the impending invasion of Europe, that SOE organized an operation called RATWEEK. All over Europe during the last week of February, 1944, SOE instructed its agents to kill as many of the senior SD staff as they could. According to Major H.J. Giskes, the head of the Abwehr counter-espionage in Holland, London ordered the assassination of twelve Dutch collaborators, the chief of the Dutch para-military organization working for the Germans and the chief of the SS. He did not say if the assassinations were carried out.

There is no record of the total number of SD personnel killed in this operation, but in one area of France an agent of the Armada circuit who was a crack shot bagged eleven senior SD men.

One aspect of agents' training seems singularly out of place and that is propaganda and political warfare. As related earlier, it was designed by Philby and taught brilliantly by himself and Paul Dehn. Philby noticed at an early date that the students showed little relish for his subject and its inclusion in the Beaulieu curriculum seems to have been the product of political infighting within SOE's high command.

At its inception SOE possessed two main branches, SO 1, its political wing, and SO 2, to carry out acts of disruption. Both were initially under the control of Hugh Dalton, who was particularly keen on the use of political methods of warfare to break the Nazis' hold over the German population as well as over their supporters in several non-belligerent European countries such as Spain and Sweden, and in their occupied territories, where, in some cases, such as several of the Russian provinces, their conquest had initially been welcomed.

SO 1 had been a brainchild of the Foreign Office and had been sponsored by the Secret Intelligence Service. It was soon hived off to a newly created outfit called the Political Warfare Executive, or PWE, which retained its close ties with the Foreign Office. It was probably out of political pique that Dalton insisted upon retaining a political and propaganda warfare element in SO 2 and insisted that Gubbins, as head of SOE training, included it as a module in the Beaulieu course.

The students were made aware of its place in the scheme of their training during the Opening Address by the Commandant, delivered soon after their arrival. Outlining the purpose of their training as Subversion, Woolrych explained that this could be achieved by various means, for instance by materially damaging the enemy's means of production and communications and by hampering his war efforts by straining his manpower resources beyond its limits, undermining his morale and by boosting the morale of the peoples of the conquered territories and inciting them to acts of resistance.

The obvious means of damaging the enemy's production capacity was by smashing the machinery of production, that is by deliberate and undisguised or 'Attributable' acts of sabotage. But this required specialist knowledge and training and would bring the Gestapo swarming into the area to find the culprits and take hostages. But inciting industrial workers to careless workmanship, teaching them to omit certain tasks such as failing to lubricate machinery, over-lubricating it, wasting precious oils, or mixing abrasives in the oil, were damaging and hard to detect, or if detected they were difficult to attribute to malintent. These were known as acts of 'Unattributable' sabotage, could be carried out with little risk to the perpetrators and were just a few of the great number of ways of damaging the enemy's war effort at little personal risk. Other ways included pedantic adherence to maintenance and safety regulations, asking for frequent inspections and overhauls 'to improve performance', directing materials to the wrong places on the production line, wasting essential and costly raw materials, in fact anything to create waste and delay. If carried out on a large scale this could seriously damage the Nazis' war effort.

Since the Germans were rounding up industrial workers and able-bodied men and women in large numbers in the occupied countries and were deporting them to Germany to work in their factories to replace their own men called up for military service, they could be made to import large numbers of unattributable saboteurs. This is why it was important for agents to teach as many people as they could how to damage the enemy's war effort with little personal risk.

The Beaulieu students needed little convincing of the relevance of this aspect of propaganda warfare, but they found political and psychological warfare very difficult to learn and very hard to swallow as a practical weapon of war. Philby related how his very first students were two Frenchmen, one of whom was Yvon Morandat, a young Christian trade unionist who became a first-rate political agitator inside occupied France and one of de Gaulle's finest political agents. They were being trained at Beaulieu for some special mission not divulged to the training staff. They became star pupils and within a fortnight were producing leaflets of a high standard. Philby said that he was mentioning it because they were almost the only trainees who took the slightest interest in politics and political propaganda.

The truth is that political and psychological warfare were very difficult and specialized subjects to master and required political direction of a very high order. Philby is known to have made numerous trips to the headquarters of the Political Warfare Executive at Woburn Abbey to gain expertise and direction. He had meetings with a well-known Fleet Street reporter of German origin, Sefton Delmer, the head of the 'Black' propaganda section.

Given political direction, it was up to the skilled propagandists and political feature writers to give topics and events damaging to the Nazi war effort a form that was acceptable to ordinary Germans and aim it at specific sections of the enemy population. There was not much point in producing defeatist news or turgid anti-Nazi political material and aiming it at Nazi bigots by way of radio broadcasts or newsprint. They would not listen to it or read it. Hence it was a matter of psychology how it was dished up to the target audience. The bigots might listen if the substance was slyly inserted into a broadcast professing to come from Nazi sources or into what appeared to be a Nazi newspaper. This is what is meant by 'Black' propaganda. It amounted to counterfeiting the source and sometimes uttering downright lies, inciting resentment by blackening the reputations of Nazi officials and even inventing Nazi officials and accusing them of corruption and embezzlement. It required huge resources, like high-powered radio transmitters, printing presses and methods of infiltrating material, and far more specialized knowledge and writing skills than most of the SOE agents were likely to possess.

Nevertheless, teaching people in the occupied countries how to commit unattributable sabotage and inciting them to go slow and commit administrative blunders did eventually pay off and did enormous damage to the Nazis' war production. There are some wonderful examples of administrative sabotage leading to the despatch of key components to far-away parts of France or Poland and causing delays of many weeks before they reached their intended destinations. In one case a distant factory that had not asked for a particularly precious component received the entire stock and very many weeks were wasted while it was being shunted about on the railways through several countries before it reached its uncalled-for destination. It took many more weeks of shunting on railways that were being bombed and sabotaged before it was returned to the original supplier.

At Beaulieu Philby, Paul Dehn and their successors taught their students how to spread damaging rumours such as circulating the story that the prostitutes in brothels reserved for Germans had been put there because they had venereal diseases, or that rat droppings had been found in the Germans' rations.

There were other, quite different acts of unattributable sabotage reported by both German and SOE sources. Powdered glass was put into the Germans' food and there are many other well-known ways of contaminating food to cause diarrhoea and intestinal infections. Powdered glass was also put into Germans clothing and SOE supplied agents with itching powder. They also supplied ampoules looking like lighter fuel capsules that contained a foul-smelling chemical which, when squirted onto clothing, caused an unremovable stench so that the clothes had to be burned to get rid of the smell. Other ampoules of chemicals were supplied which, if ingested, produced the symptoms of serious diseases. These were given or sold to disgruntled German soldiers wishing to avoid postings to the Russian front or seeking a discharge from the army on medical grounds.

Chapter X

SURVIVAL, SECURITY AND RESISTANCE TO INTERROGATION

The Survival, Security and Resistance to Interrogation training that the students received at Beaulieu was fundamentally incompatible with their commando, sabotage and spycraft training and it was left to the students, when qualified as agents, to reconcile the two areas and strike their own balance. Too much emphasis on security meant they would achieve very little; too little and they did not survive for very long.

As the official report on agent training emphasized, training the students to lead clandestine lives was not so much a matter of training them in spycrafts as inculcating a habit of mind, the habit of constant vigilance and attention to matters of security. Failure to adopt this mentality would quickly lead to their arrest and would also hazard the lives of others in their circuits. And after they had been arrested those who failed to remember their resistance to interrogation training would jeopardize others if they spoke too soon, even under torture, and if not tortured they might be easily tricked into revealing far more of consequence than they realized. As we shall see, the subject of interrogation is far more complex than being simply a matter of devising ways to force information out of a prisoner, or even of framing pertinent questions and seeking flaws in the answers.

Throughout the entire period of the School's existence the principal instructor in Survival training was Captain William Clark, who was also the 'Housemaster' at The Vineyards. He often expressed his doubts about the value of teaching Living Off the Land to people who were to become urban guerrillas and is said to have objected to the use of women as agents. Whatever his misgivings he would have been pleased to know that, although he was the least educated of the Beaulieu instructors, he was by far the best remembered. Every Beaulieu-trained agent who later wrote about his or her experiences invariably mentioned him by name and remembered his lessons in survival.

All the students who had come from the SOE commando school at Arisaig had learned to crawl about the countryside inconspicuously, to walk silently on various surfaces, to map-read and survive a soaking in a desolate area of Scotland. But they knew that at the end of the day they would be returning to barracks and a hot meal. Their survival training at Beaulieu was meant to teach them to support themselves for longer periods and to live alone off the land for weeks on end should events compel them to do so.

'Nobby' was surprisingly light on his feet and there was little he did not know about silently stalking game or people without frightening flocks of rooks and other birds into flight to warn of his presence. He taught his students far more about fieldcraft than they had learned at the commando school, also how to snare rabbits, catch game and hedgehogs, to fish and to sustain themselves with fruit, herbs, berries, stinging nettles and other vegetation growing in the wild. He also taught them how to steal chickens and livestock without alerting the owners with their cries, to steal root crops and other cultivated edibles, to prepare all kinds of meat and food for the pot, and how to make smokeless fires. One of the lessons frequently mentioned by former agents is catching and cooking hedge-hogs, which are apparently good to eat and are abundant in the New Forest. After killing them they would be coated with a thick layer of clay before being placed in the embers of a fire. When cooked, the clay would be removed taking with it all the skin and bristles. He taught his students how to shoot game as well as snare it, and to fish with 'stun grenades' made of quicklime and water!

His students had to learn how to make hides in various kinds of countryside and were compelled to spend a night or two in them in the open. They had to learn to sleep and live rough and be presentable after doing so. Whether many of the students found these lessons of practical use after they had been parachuted into occupied Europe is not known.

Training in security was an integral part of the lessons on Agent Management and Techniques and practical lessons in many aspects of security were incorporated into all the schemes, including losing a 'tail', arranging cells and cut-outs and dead letter boxes, personal security and warning signals. There were many aspects that could be taught and prac-tised in-house, including disguises. Another was how to detect whether one's room had been searched in one's absence. The students were constantly reminded of the importance of being meticulously tidy so that they would notice if any of their belongings had been disturbed. They were also taught how to lay inconspicuous traps on their bedroom doors and to scatter them over their belongings, devices like using talcum powder, cigarette ash, laying hairs or threads across places likely to be searched, and placing minute pieces of paper, pieces of matchsticks or leaves in door jambs and in the cheeks of drawers so that they would drop out if they were opened. While the students were out of their rooms, the rooms would be searched by Field Security or other members of the staff who knew all the tricks and would replace the traps to see if the students would still notice that their rooms had been searched.

Students were implored never to commit anything to paper, but in case they needed to do so they were taught to conceal compromising equipment and materials within a room. Although it is doubtful if any novice agent could find a hiding place in a room that would defeat a trained team of spycatchers, there are many places that would escape a perfunctory search or even a more thorough search by soldiers and others who had not been specially trained. It was necessary to teach the students to avoid using hoary old ruses like sticking things under a mattress or on the undersides of drawers and suspending things in the old-fashioned high-level lavatory cisterns. Better to use the insides of electrical appliances and wireless sets where a searcher would think twice about searching to avoid being electrocuted or in the pipe that holds the hangers in a wardrobe or in a small hole drilled into the top of an internal door or to remove an internal door mortice lock, use the cavity for storage and replace the lock. On operations many agents carried large sums of money in cash and bundles of forged documents. Where they hid them is not recorded, but these were probably buried in gardens or fields. No doubt the SOE factory was able to supply special equipment, such as shoes with hollow heels, toothpaste tubes and talcum powder containers with storage space and even hollowed out chessmen, for hiding small compromising articles, especially during transit.

Students had to devise their own sets of warning signals, that is inconspicuous but unambiguous signs that would warn off others or inform them that it was safe to approach a premises. These signs included flowers, dusters and a variety of objects left in front room windows, curtains and blinds pulled in a certain way, doormats left askew, a thread of wool hanging from a door handle, matchsticks and leaves laid in certain ways; the variations were endless. The problem for the students was to remember their own signals and what they meant.

There was a long list of quite elementary precautions that the students had to learn, like don't share accommodation with another agent, or commit anything to writing, or talk about operations; don't go directly to meetings or sit in a public vehicle; stand near the exit. Don't disclose the name on your identity card or carry more than one identity card. Don't get drunk in public or chase the girls or sleep with another agent. (Two agents of the French Section are said to have been caught in bed together when arrested – although they denied it – professing afterwards to their captors that they really were husband and wife). And don't use a two-way dead letter box or somebody may use it to trap you.

Despite all their security training many agents were incredibly careless when they went on operations and were soon caught because they made the most elementary mistakes. The prime example was the arrest of the entire French National Council for Resistance as they assembled in one house on the outskirts of Lyon in June, 1943. One famous radio-operator of the French Section, Noor Inayat Khan, was particularly careless on matters of security and received an adverse report at the end of her training at Beaulieu. Nevertheless, she was sent on operations and, when betrayed, the Germans found not only her radio set but in the drawer of her bedside table was an exercise book in which she had recorded in cypher and in plain language every message she had sent and received! She died a terrible death in a concentration camp.

The subject of Resistance to Interrogation may seem to the uninitiated a matter of keeping one's mouth shut in the face of persistent questioning under unspeakable tortures. The ultimate form of resistance was the cyanide pill with which every agent was supplied for use if captured. How many of them chose this method of denying the Gestapo operational information is not known. Short of committing suicide there were in fact several things the agents could do besides braving torture to delay or deny the enemy information.

Training in resistance to interrogation has a history dating back to the First World War when our troops were instructed that if captured they were to reveal only their names, rank and number in accordance with the terms of the Geneva Convention. By the outbreak of the Second World War there had been a number of advances in interrogation technology (by which I do NOT mean appliances of torture) which rendered the name, rank and number policy inadequate. Nevertheless, the troops were still indoctrinated in the use of this simple policy and, in addition, were told that if captured it was their duty to try to escape so as to tie down as many enemy personnel as possible in trying to prevent them from doing so and wasting personnel hunting for them if they succeeded. A selected few from all three services, especially aircrew and special service personnel, were given training by an outfit that called itself IS 9 (Intelligence School No.9) in codes, how to organize escapes from prison camps, what was available in the way of escape devices and how these could be introduced into the prison camps.

The majority of our service personnel were not told that a new secret service, MI 9, had been created to organize and run escape lines to help them get away. Worldwide, MI 9 rescued 33,758 evaders and escapers, 12,112 of them from Western Europe; almost half of these were brought out through Switzerland. An interesting statistic is that more officers than Other Ranks evaded capture and more Other Ranks than officers escaped from captivity. The larger number of OR escapers is due to the fact that they were obliged to do work for the Germans outside their prison camps, giving them a better opportunity to escape.

IS 9 was a part of MI 9 and taught servicemen what it called Conduct after Capture, which included resistance to interrogation. MI 9 was itself part of the Prisoner of War Intelligence Directorate, the other half of which was MI 19, which was responsible for interrogating enemy prisoners of war. And it was MI 19 that provided the expertise for training servicemen to resist interrogation and from whom SOE obtained their information for training the students to resist some of the more important aspects of interrogation. These aspects, considered to be top secret at the time, remained so until 1961 when they were revealed in the report of the Privy Council Committee on Interrogation Procedures, the so-called Parker Committee, after its chairman Lord Parker of Waddington. They included the routine use of concealed microphones and stool pigeons. A stool pigeon is a witting or unwitting informer inserted into a prisoner group or into the cell of an isolated prisoner to encourage him or her to talk carelessly.

MI 19 was staffed with experts in the use of these techniques, and it was discovered that the Germans were also using them in their interrogation centres, especially in Dulag Luft, through which they processed captured Allied aircrews.

The use of stool pigeons is a very ancient aspect of interrogation and their use in conjunction with microphones requires a re-definition of the common concept of interrogation.

The popular definition is that it is a process of overt, close, confrontational questioning by an identifiable interrogator empowered to punish his victim for failure to respond. But in fact there is no divine edict which impels an interrogator to reveal his identity as such nor any compulsion to question a suspect in a blatant manner or in circumstances indicative of interrogation. The exclusive use of the confrontational form of interrogation is regarded by many professionals as the hallmark of the amateur and inferior to a number of more subtle methods of 'questioning', including the use of the forensic sciences.

Interrogation can be regarded as a state of mind in the person interrogated. Carried out officiously in formal or threatening circumstances, close questioning will be perceived as an interrogation. Effected in a pleasant manner in either formal or informal surroundings, it will be seen as an interview. Conducted in a café or in a club by an acquaintance or by somebody posing as a friend, it may be perceived as an interesting discussion! Yet the same questions may be asked in all three settings. Therefore why hurl oneself at a barricaded front door if there is an option of sneaking round the back? Better still, tap interestingly at the front door while simultaneously effecting an entry at the back, in effect using direct and threatening interrogation as a cover for the use of more subtle methods in innocuous circumstances.

The recruitment, placement and control of the human agent is the nub of the professional interrogator's skill as well as that of a detective. The human agent, the informer or stool pigeon does not necessarily realize that he or she is being used as such. The study of the experiences of captured agents shows that there were at least four varieties of stool pigeons used by the Germans. The first was a 'friendly' guard, doctor, nurse or some other 'enemy' official, or an interrogator posing as one, not associated in the prisoner's mind with the interrogation team, who pretends sympathy while acting as an agent. The second was the specially trained enemy agent, sometimes known as a penetration agent, who poses as a member of the prisoner's organization or social set injected into the suspect's company in a fashion that does not arouse suspicion. The third was a volunteer from among the suspect's acquaintances who, for whatever reasons, agreed to help the interrogators. The Germans promised to spare their lives in exchange for their help but executed them nonetheless once they had served their purposes. The fourth type was an acquaintance of the suspect's who did not realize that he or she was being used. Types 2, 3 and 4 can be described as clandestine methods of interrogation.

Being a stool pigeon or informer of any category could be a dangerous occupation; mere suspicion was often enough to prompt revenge. If discovered or even suspected of being one, they ran the risk of being beaten up or murdered. There was an instance of a particularly ruthless group of imprisoned (post-war) terrorists using the corner of an iron bedstead to smash the skull of a member of their group suspected of being an SP. Next morning when the murder was discovered, the culprits commented, 'Oh dear! What a pity! He must have fallen and hit his head when he got up for a pee during the night!'

It was not unknown for interrogators to throw suspicion on to an innocent party in order to protect the real SP, or to throw suspicion on to the leader of an intractable group in order to destroy the group's cohesion and get them quarrelling among themselves so that they would talk carelessly in the presence of stool pigeons or microphones. Throwing suspicion on to a prisoner is easily achieved by calling the victim to more frequent interrogations than the remainder of his group and showing him special favours, like giving him cigarettes or chocolate to take back to his cell each time he is called.

The term 'stool pigeon' is usually applied to agents used during captivity. But identical types of agents or informers were used on suspects at any time before they were arrested, if indeed they were arrested. They were sometimes left free to lead the counter-espionage agents to other members of the suspect's circle of acquaintances.

Manoeuvring the suspect into a situation where he or she could be made vulnerable to indirect or clandestine methods, even specially creating suitable situations, is part and parcel of the interrogator's art. It includes continuing interrogation long after the suspect thinks that it has been completed, long after he or she has been removed from an identifiable interrogation centre to, for instance, a common gaol. These kinds of interrogations through a second party, or by creating a 'sting' situation, or continuing during a prison sentence, are omitted from the common concept of interrogation which places total emphasis upon the art of direct questioning by an identifiable interrogator in an identifiable place of interrogation.

Wartime training in resistance to interrogation included warning servicemen to watch out for stool pigeons and hidden microphones. The training at Beaulieu included these warnings, but it in no way prepared the students to identify stool pigeons, nor were they alerted to the possibility that the entire group of acquaintances or 'fellow prisoners' might be stool pigeons. Similarly the students were not shown what a microphone looked like, where they were likely to be hidden, how to recognize the circumstances when they were most likely to be used, or how to defeat them by making a background noise to cover whispered conversations. Nor were the trainees warned that every single room or cell or communal room, including the lavatories, were likely to be monitored. People tended to think that microphones, if used, would be used singly rather than in batteries scattered generously all over the place irrespective of the cost and the number of listeners required to do the monitoring.

The microphones used in those days were not recognizable as such to the uninitiated. They did not contain transmitters and batteries as they do today but were wired directly to the listening room. They and their wires were usually hidden. If left visible the microphone resembled a sandwich of bakelite wafers less than a quarter of an inch thick and an inch square and looked like an insignificant component of an ancient wireless set. The only thing about them to arouse a layman's curiosity was the two thin wires trailing out of the device. They could be hidden in overhead lights and skirting boards and other fixtures and fittings in a room. It needed a small orifice about an inch long and the width of a twopenny piece to let in the sound and could not, therefore, be buried in wall plaster.

As far as is known none of the Beaulieu staff had served in MI 19. The security experts came from Field Security which did not include in its training the use of concealed microphones or the recruitment, control and placement of stool pigeons and all the problems that go with the expert use and control of such devices. The uninitiated might think that microphones are simple to use, but anybody who has tried to use one will know that they create many problems. They are 'blind' and 'dumb' and, unlike stool pigeons, cannot react by asking questions based upon the information received. They cannot be used in every kind of acoustic environment which means in effect that rooms in which they are used have to be specially built, or specially selected for their acoustics. The older type of microphones were non-directional, leading to problems in identifying the person who was speaking; their lack of clarity also made it hard to identify the speaker. They also posed problems of 'real time' listening. In those days acoustic activation of recording equipment had not been invented and an hour of recorded conversation took an hour to play back. Also, anybody who has tried making a live recording will know that much of what is recorded is trivial and of no consequence and several people tend to speak at the same time, making it impossible to untangle who is speaking about what. The novice listener is likely to listen with a pair of headphones all day and not hear anything of significance, which is a waste of time and incurs a massive loss of vigilance.

The task of routine listening would have been delegated to signals personnel who would have had to be briefed on what matters to listen for and record.

126

In those days the recording equipment was archaic by today's standards, but both disc and tape recording equipment had long been invented and Germany had the lead in the development of sound recording equipment.

Disc equipment comprised immensely heavy turntables supporting heavy wax discs revolving at 72 rpm. The disc would only record for a short period and hours of conversation would have occupied a pile of discs. The listener would have had to cut a wax disc by lowering the cutting arm on to the disc at the appropriate moment and later the recording would have had to be played back on a gramophone and interesting passages marked on the disc with a coloured pencil! Tape recorders had been invented by the Germans in 1929. Earlier German versions had used wire instead of magnetic tape. Tape recordings were first used by the BBC in 1932. After the Germans had been defeated, the Allies discovered that they had made significant advances in the development of magnetic tape-recording equipment and eighteen pieces of this equipment were seized as reparations. Reel-to-reel tape recorders did not become widely available until the 1950s and stereo decks did not appear until the 1970s.

Whatever type of recording equipment was in use during the war, it was imperative that the listener was highly discriminating in what he placed on record so as to avoid the tedium of real-time playback of hours of useless chatter. By implication he would have had to get to know his suspect's habits so well that he could guess at what time of day and under what circumstances he was most likely to talk about matters of significance.

Clearly an intelligent interrogator would not waste his time on passive listening. He would study his suspect carefully and manipulate circumstances so as to cause him to confide to his cell mate, who would, of course, have been specially chosen for the purpose, at a convenient time. Equally clearly an interrogator would also have had to have known how to plant and to extricate a stool pigeon for de-briefing and re-briefing and how to put him back again without arousing suspicion.

The overwhelming evidence about the Beaulieu instruction in resistance to interrogation indicates that it stuck to the traditional, antiquated view and gave undue emphasis to the duel of wits and close questioning, to the exclusion of the hidden dangers. Exercises in resistance included some duress. Dressed in Abwehr, SS or SD uniforms, members of the instructor staff barged into the students' bedrooms in the middle of the night, woke them, hauled them into another room and made them stand in their night attire with their arms above their heads, holding a pile of heavy books or telephone directories while bombarding them with questions to test their endurance and their cover stories. Later in the war the male students were also subjected to the indignity of strip searches and were made to stand naked in the cold while being questioned. There is no record of women students being subjected to such treatment nor is there any evidence of the students ever being subjected to the indecency of a body search, though they were told to expect them if captured.

In his book *SOE 1940–46*, M.R.D. Foot stated that in 1943 some of the bedrooms in some of the Beaulieu houses were wired for sound in order to discover if the students talked in their sleep and, if so, in what language. If microphones were used in this way, it was an inexpert use of this facility and would have created problems of real-time listening. Some unfortunate member of the staff, probably a Field Security corporal, would have been stuck on the end of a pair of headphones for countless nights on end on the offchance of hearing something useful. Foot also stated that prior to the installation of microphones a 'devastating blonde' named Fifi was used as a stool pigeon to find out if the students talked in their sleep; presumably Fifi was used only on the male students! Some former agents said that seductive women or attractive men were used on them during their field exercises to chat them up on park benches or in pubs to see if they would reveal more than they should. It is known that these questioners were the female secretaries and the male staff of the school, most probably Field Security personnel.

The Beaulieu students were taught that if caught by the Gestapo or the Abwehr they were to endeavour at all cost to conceal operational matters for at least forty-eight hours, to give others time to disappear. They were also told that, even if captured by the Gestapo, all was not lost because the Gestapo men were mostly thugs not noted for their wits and showed little in the way of subtlety and finesse. Some of them could be bribed or blackmailed. In truth, the Gestapo men were often as inexperienced in interrogation as the agents were inexperienced in escaping their attention, and there are many examples of agents outwitting them under questioning and some instances of the interrogators accepting bribes and permitting the release of the suspect. There are one or two examples, late in the war, of them being blackmailed into releasing agents. There are also many examples, far too many, of them torturing their victims to death rather than keeping them alive and trying more subtle ways of making them reveal valuable information.

The Abwehr interrogators do not seem to have been quite so brutal and they were marginally more proficient at the more subtle methods of interrogation than were their rivals in the Gestapò. The evidence suggests that German army officers regarded the task of interrogation with distaste and thought it was unsuitable work for decent officers. Several of their most proficient spycatchers were NCOs.

Chapter XI

WHAT THE GERMANS KNEW

How much did the Germans know about Beaulieu and how did they find out? The Gestapo and the Abwehr interrogators liked to give their captives the impression that they knew everything, but this is an ancient interrogators' ploy. They were also fond of bragging that they had an agent located in a senior position in SOE's headquarters in Baker Street. Were these claims justified?

The spycatchers' dream is not simply to catch spies piecemeal and render them harmless by shooting them or imprisoning them, but to use them to obtain as much information as possible about their operations and techniques and, ideally, to 'work them back' to their spymasters to the point where the spycatchers take control of the spymasters' operations. Our own counter-espionage agency, MI 5, did this very successfully to the German spies in this country during the war. It was known as 'The Double Cross System'.

The Germans never managed to do the same to us on the same scale, but they did manage to take control of the operations of the Dutch Section of SOE for an extensive period at the cost of the lives of fifty-five Dutch agents before that Section became fully aware of what was happening. It was a feat which they were unable to repeat on the same scale in any of the other occupied countries, although they tried repeatedly and with modest success. They called the Dutch coup 'Operation Nordpol' and it is a classic example of how the Germans obtained quantities of intelligence about SOE's operations and a great deal of information about the training of the agents. It was a 'sting' operation involving sixty German and Dutch personnel, among them collaborators who acted as penetration agents, 'turned' spies, about half a dozen skilful German signalmen to operate the very clever 'play back' of SOE radio sets and the use of overt and clandestine interrogation techniques.

Much of the information which the Germans garnered from this operation was handed to them on a plate without resorting to violent methods and it shows how easily the agents, many of whom were very young, could be tricked into revealing almost everything despite all the security training they had been given at Beaulieu and elsewhere. Many of the captured agents were promised that their lives would be spared if they assisted their captors and many of them did so. But in November, 1943, fifty-five imprisoned agents were shot on the orders of the Gestapo in an attempt to keep Operation Nordpol a secret.

Nordpol lasted from February, 1942, to December, 1943, and spilt over into SOE's and MI 9's circuits in Belgium and northern France. After the war there were bitter recriminations about the Dutch débâcle and both the Dutch and the British authorities launched high-level investigations into how Nordpol was allowed to continue for so long without the Dutch Section and the headquarters staff of SOE being aware of what was happening. Searching questions were asked. Why had the British and Dutch controlling officers failed to notice the absence of an array of security checks in the radio transmissions of such a large number of agents under German control? Where had the Germans obtained so much detailed intelligence that was necessary to hoodwink the Section in the first instance? How had they managed to break and use the appropriate codes? How had they contrived to use a style of language in the decoded messages which replicated what SOE expected to receive from their own agents? How had they managed to continue it at the cost of so many lives? Had the Germans been assisted by a German agent within the upper echelons of SOE, as they had claimed? And why had the Dutch Section's officers refused to accept that the worst had happened even when they had received information to that effect from various sources, including the testimonies of five of their own agents who had escaped from the Gestapo? Two of these escapers had managed to reach Britain with the news and had warned their superiors of the Germans' claim to have an agent within SOE. Why had their information been ignored and why had they been consigned to Brixton prison as suspected double agents? Had they been imprisoned to conceal the existence of a German spy within SOE?

The German officer who was largely responsible for the devastation of the Dutch operations was a 47-year-old former tobacco salesman, H.J. Giskes, a major in the Abwehr, who had been called up for active service in 1938. He had been involved with some sort of military intelligence for some years previously. At first he worked with the Abwehr Section of the

OKW, the German High Command, under Admiral Canaris. In 1940 he was working in counter-espionage in Paris and a year later moved to The Hague to do similar work. In 1943 he became the Chief of Military Counter-Espionage for Holland, Belgium and northern France. He was eventually captured by the Allies and held as a prisoner of war until September, 1948, three and a half years after the end of the war, when, presumably, the Allies were satisfied that they had wrung him dry of every scrap of useful information about his wartime activities.

In 1953 Giskes published his memoirs and in them he mentions that in Holland he had been compelled to work closely with his counterpart in the Gestapo, a major in the SD by the name of J. Schreieder, who possessed the usual Gestapo powers over all other German personnel but lacked the personal experience and the trained personnel to locate and 'play back' captured radio sets. Schreieder had therefore been forced to turn for help to Giskes and the Abwehr for the 'play back' radio operators, without whose skills he could not exploit captured wireless operators or run an operation like Nordpol.

The pair of them benefited greatly from the skills of the Abwehr radio-location service and signals personnel and also from the skill of an Abwehr sergeant by the name of E. May, whom one of his victims described as 'a typical Prussian, corpulent, hair clipped, short in stature, never impatient, friendly, never excited and notoriously thorough'. May was not only a skilful interrogator but he was also an expert with British codes and security checks.

It has frequently been alleged that SOE sent amateur agents into the field to face the professional spycatchers of the Gestapo and the Abwehr. The fact that about 60% or more of SOE's agents in Europe were never caught is sufficient evidence that the German counter-espionage services were not as professional as some people have suggested, especially when compared with the successes of MI 5 in this country. The reality is that the Germans were just as amateur as anybody else who had been called up for duty during the war. They had to learn by experience. Only in Holland did their counter-espionage services meet with a high degree of success, perhaps because of the exceptional degree of cooperation between Giskes of the Abwehr and Schreieder of the SD. Elsewhere in Europe the two organizations were bitter rivals and refused to share their information. Most of the Gestapo men had been recruited for their youthful devotion to Nazism and for their familiarity with the criminal underworld and not for their knowledge or experience of intelligence work. Very few of them were properly trained for spycatching or interrogation, usually relying on torture, strictly adhering to the orders of Himmler, who was Chief of the despicable SS. Those chilling orders stated that the enemies of the Führer:-

'should die, certainly, but not before torture, indignity and interrogation has drained from them the last shred and scintilla of evidence which should lead to the arrest of others. Then and only then should the blessed release of death be granted to them.'

This makes Schreieder's restraint in Holland and his co-operation with the Abwehr all the more remarkable. He is reputed to have been ordered by a higher authority in the Gestapo to accept Giskes' subtle approach in the interests of exploiting the success of Nordpol.

The methods which they employed to catch the SOE agents in Holland were routine counter-espionage techniques such as the monitoring and control of all modes of communication, control of peoples' movements, snap checks, using trained surveillance agents to do the watching and detectives to do the detecting, deploying penetration agents, creating networks of sub-agents, collaborators and informers, offering large rewards for information and encouraging citizens to report anything suspicious. But the most telling technique of all was sustained monitoring of the air waves for unauthorized transmissions, recording them and deploying radio-location teams to pinpoint the location of the illegal operatives.

In Holland, as elsewhere in occupied Europe, the Germans had sympathizers and collaborators among the native population to assist their investigation and take active parts as Nazi agents. Some of the people who assisted the Abwehr and the Gestapo had no doubt been inherited from the Dutch equivalent of our Criminal Investigation Department. Others were inducted by the threat of criminal proceedings for breaches of the numerous German occupation regulations. Using these routine methods both the Gestapo and the Abwehr had managed to catch a number of Dutch SOE agents before the start of Nordpol.

Giskes first successes came at the end of 1941 through his use of a shady Dutch diamond merchant and opium smuggler who volunteered his services as an Abwehr informer. This man, Ridderhoff, was a large, powerfully built individual of about 40 years of age, with a winning personality and a gift of worming his way into peoples' confidence. He discovered that British agents had been dropped into a particular locality, were busy creating a widespread resistance organization and were looking for sites for air drops of arms. At first Giskes disbelieved him because the Abwehr radio location service had not detected any unauthorized transmissions. He discounted the report as rumour and told his subordinates to take their stories to the North Pole. Thus the origins of the name Nordpol.

In January, 1942, Schreieder's men of the SD caught a radio operator, but none of them had sufficient knowledge to work the prisoner or the skill to play back the radio. That same month three Dutch agents were caught awaiting evacuation by a British MTB and the Abwehr radio monitors located and recorded the transmissions of a Dutch SOE agent. Ridderhoff's information was therefore validated and the Abwehr and its radio location service were alerted and began systematic searches of the air waves for further illegal transmissions.

When the RAF dropped the first consignment of arms for the Dutch Resistance on 28 February, 1942, Ridderhoff was present, probably as a member of a reception committee. One week later the Abwehr radio location service located an SOE radio operator by the name of Lauwers and he was arrested and his radio set seized. Lauwers was compelled to use his transmitter under Abwehr instructions and, although he used his security checks to alert his SOE controllers to his capture, the officers of the Dutch Section failed to notice anything irregular about the transmissions. And so began Operation Nordpol which would not have been possible had the Germans not already possessed a great deal of information about SOE's operational techniques and exact knowledge of the identities of the Dutch Section controllers and their methods of control.

By the autumn numerous agents had already fallen into the trap and the Germans were playing back fourteen captured radio sets which were being operated by half a dozen Abwehr signalmen who were able to replicate the transmitting style or 'fist' of the captured operators. Sergeant E. May had managed to break their codes and had knowledge of the system of security checks. Giskes and Schreieder knew the names and appearances of every officer in the Dutch Section of SOE, knew all the schools the agents had attended and knew the names and appearances of many of the instructors in the schools.

Some of the methods they used to acquire this information is revealed in the story of Sergeant Pieter Dourlein, one of the escapers who risked his life to bring the news to Britain. He was a young Dutch radio operator who had been recruited into SOE from the Royal Netherlands Navy in which he had served as a Leading Seaman in a warship in the Far East. Upon his transfer to SOE he had undergone the usual courses of commando and parachute training before being sent to Beaulieu. He had been parachuted into Holland with two other agents, Bogaart and Arendse, and a radio set, in March, 1943, a year after the start of Nordpol, straight into the laps of the awaiting German agents. On landing the trio were met by six Dutchmen, all of whom were working for the Germans as a bogus reception committee. The SOE agents were greeted with their correct code names and were treated to cigarettes and whisky. The suspicions of the new arrivals were only slightly aroused when they were asked to hand over their weapons on the excuse that if they kept them they would compromise themselves if stopped and searched. They were also asked to reveal their real names and, after conferring with each other, they supplied them, which was strictly against all the security rules they had been taught at Beaulieu and elsewhere. This request alone should have thoroughly aroused their suspicions. Already relieved of their weapons, they were separated and each was accompanied by two members of the reception committee. Soon afterwards each of the SOE agents was hand-cuffed by their pair of minders. Whistles were blown, more Dutchmen appeared and they were taken in separate cars to a local security centre.

Many earlier agents who had fallen into the Nordpol trap had been taken to a supposed 'safe house', which was in fact a German hide-out, and for two days were kept talking to members of the bogus reception committee about their mission before being arrested. The amount of information the Germans obtained by this simple ruse must have been enormous, especially if the 'safe house' had been equipped with microphones and recorders, which is highly probable.

After his arrest Dourlein was searched and taken before 'a short plump German in civvies' who immediately picked up a matchbox containing a false bottom in which was concealed the address of a Swiss safe house, and removed this information. At this very first session his interrogator told Dourlein at which schools he had received his training in the last six months, correct in every detail, and mentioned a number of Dutch and English controllers and instructors by name. He was sufficiently familiar with their appearances, mannerisms and roles to sound convincing. He casually enquired after many of the Beaulieu instructors by name as if they were old friends of his! He concluded, 'We know it all. You see, we have our own people in England and I'm sure you know them too!'

Unlike the trainers in our Secret Intelligence Service, the SOE trainers never adopted false names or changed aliases to suite every occasion. They were known to all their students by their real names.

Dourlein's interrogator seemed to know so much that by the time he had finished his questioning Dourlein was convinced that his claim to have an agent in SOE's headquarters was true. After two hours of independent questioning the three agents were transported to the Gestapo prison at Haaren and handed over to Sergeant E. May of the Abwehr.

May had Dourlein thoroughly searched and then began to question him. Like many other captured agents, Dourlein must have felt very foolish about falling into the trap of telling the members of his reception committee about his mission. It was too late to retract when confronted with a formal interrogation. When he refused to cooperate May took him on the tour of the cells where he was shown forty Dutch agents and asked if he recognized any of them. It was an obvious ploy to demoralize the prisoner thoroughly and it had the intended effect.

Like many other agents faced with the prospect of death, Dourlein's mind must have raced over the various ways of placating his captors and saving his life. In this situation many SOE agents immediately revealed all they knew. Others were talked into offering their services as double agents or stool pigeons in exchange for their lives, but those who accepted were eventually executed despite the promises they had been given. Yet others played for time, pretending to cooperate by revealing substantial amounts of non-operational information. There were two subjects that could always be used to give the impression of being cooperative without jeopardizing the lives of others. One was to talk about themselves. The other was to talk at length about the training they had received, the schools they had attended and about the instructors. Each scrap of information added to the store of information used by the interrogators to convince later arrivals that they did indeed know everything. In interrogation knowledge breeds knowledge.

Sergeant May questioned Dourlein with endless patience about his signalling routines and codes and after forty hours of non-stop questioning allowed his prisoner to go to his cell to sleep for a brief period before the questioning was resumed. During the weeks that followed they exchanged information about sabotage techniques and sometimes May spoke about the training at Beaulieu and in Scotland. Dourlein also implies that they talked at length about how he had escaped from Holland after the German occupation and about his life in Britain and in the Dutch Navy before being recruited into SOE. Like all escapers from the continent to Britain after the German occupation of their countries, Dourlein had been cleared through the MI 5 security establishment, the Royal Patriotic School, a former girls' school on the outskirts of London. May seemed to be particularly interested in this establishment and had

Dourlein draw plans of its layout as well as discussing details of the clearance system. There could be only one reason for his interest and that was to see if it was possible for the Germans to get an agent posing as a refugee through the school undetected.

During the six weeks of his overt interrogation Dourlein was never assaulted or in any way physically abused. He was kept in solitary confinement, fed quite well and allowed a ration of tobacco. The reasonable treatment he had received in the Gestapo prison at Haaren was later to be used by British security interrogators as evidence of his cooperation with his captors. Admittedly the Haaren régime was quite uncharacteristic of the usual treatment of prisoners held in Gestapo prisons. Nearby there was a concentration camp where the SS guards were beating Dutchmen to death.

On completion of his overt interrogation Dourlein was moved to another cell where he was joined by his associate Bogaart.

It is a fair assumption that the Germans were doing what they were doing in Dulag Luft, that is using hidden microphones and stool pigeons in their detailed interrogation centres and in the special wings of their prisons. Certainly Dourlein and Bogaart would not have been reunited for humane or charitable reasons. After lengthy solitary confinement and all the tensions that build up in people expecting torture and death, they must have been bursting to exchange experiences and confidences, probably chattered eagerly and at length to check out with each other what they had told their interrogators, forgetting all their resistance to interrogation training, to the benefit of their listeners.

Two months later, when they had probably exhausted conversation about anything new, they were transferred to another cell where they were joined by a third prisoner, Van der Bor, another captured agent. It was while they were in this cell that Dourlein began talking to his cellmates about escaping and made contact with Jan Ubbink who was in an adjacent cell. Whispering to each other through a hole they had made in the adjoining wall, under a sink, they began plotting their escape. Had these cells possessed concealed microphones the Germans would have heard Dourlein talking to his cellmates about escaping and they might have heard the whispering with Ubbink. They would have taken steps to separate and punish the plotters before they made their escape. The fact that the pair conversed in whispers indicates that they had at last remembered something about their training in resistance to interrogation.

The pair squeezed themselves through the skylights over their cell doors, hid all day in a cubicle of a lavatory used by the guards and that night, 29/30 August, 1943, during a thunderstorm, lowered themselves with a rope made from bedding to the ground forty feet below and disappeared.

They hid in a house within a stone's throw of the prison and two weeks later went to the town of Tilburg in the south of Holland and remained there for months before attempting to leave the country. They were helped to get away from Tilburg by a former police inspector who, earlier in the war, had collaborated with the Nazis, a fact which the British security interrogators were later to use as evidence that the Germans had assisted their escape to Britain to work as double agents. The inspector was later assassinated by the Dutch underground.

Eventually they reached Berne, after wandering through Belgium and France, and reported to the British Embassy. Here they reported that the Germans were controlling all the Dutch SOE operations and radio transmissions and had captured all the agents. London ordered them to be sent to England by 'a safe route' which turned out to be an escape line through France into Spain, reaching there on 1 December. They were shipped to Gibraltar from where they were flown to an airfield near Bristol on 1 February, 1944. Two days later they were sent to London for debriefing by a British Intelligence officer, to whom they reported that the entire Dutch operation had been compromised and was under German control and that the Germans claimed to have an agent within SOE.

They were not believed and were sent to a holding camp for returning agents near Guildford where they discovered they were virtually under arrest. There were three other Dutchmen being held with them in the same camp. One of them was not really a Dutch national but a Field Security sergeant of the Intelligence Corps who spoke impeccable Dutch and was acting as an agent for British security.

Sergeant H.G. Fleming, the British agent, was multi-lingual; he spoke flawless Dutch and fluent French and German. He had been recruited into SOE in October, 1943, after years of service in Field Security in Britain, America and Jamaica. After joining SOE, he had spent three months training with student agents at the commando school in Scotland, had learned to parachute with them at Ringway and had been with them through an explosives course at Hereford, to prepare him for the role of a Conducting Officer. He had been posted to Guildford to 'look after' the four Dutchmen being held under suspicion and had been asked to pose as one of their fellow countrymen.

Graham Fleming had an extraordinary background. His mother was

Dutch but his father was an Englishman who, during the First World War, had been sent with a naval brigade to defend besieged Antwerp. When the defence collapsed under a German assault the brigade retreated into Holland, a neutral country. Members of the brigade who had thrown away their arms during the retreat were immediately repatriated by boat to Folkestone. But those who had kept their weapons were interned for the rest of the war! Among the internees was Fleming senior. He remained there so long that he learned to speak Dutch fluently and married a Dutch woman with whom he had a family.

After the war Fleming senior could not get a job in England but was able to get one as a representative in Holland. His son, Graham, went to a Dutch school and later to a Dutch college and took a job in the Netherlands. He was virtually Dutch.

When Holland was over-run by the Germans during the Second World War Graham escaped to England and sought refuge with relatives in Bristol. He volunteered as aircrew but the RAF failed to respond for months. Meantime he had seen an advertisement in the press saying that the army required linguists and volunteered his services. At the age of twenty-two he signed on, was interviewed by an army officer and sent home before being called to a depot in Avonmouth to be kitted out. Although he had received no military training whatever, he was told to sew on the stripe of a lance corporal. He had been recruited into the Field Security Police, later to become the Field Security Wing of the Intelligence Corps. Thereafter his army career followed a similar course to those of Bill Brooker, Cuthbert Skilbeck and many others who had volunteered their linguistic skills to the army.

Typically for those times, Fleming received no basic army training or any training in military Intelligence matters or interrogation techniques before being assigned to the docks to vet the crews of incoming merchant vessels, looking for infiltrators and collecting whatever useful Intelligence he could.

He was promoted to the rank of sergeant within a year and, after two years in Avonmouth, he was sent via America to Jamaica for a purpose that was not to be revealed to him for many weeks. Eventually a shipload of Jewish refugees from the Netherlands arrived and he was put among them to keep an eye on them, scarcely a taxing occupation and one that seemed to have nothing whatever to do with the war in Europe. He had great difficulty in obtaining a posting back to England, and when he eventually returned to the Intelligence Corps depot in Rotherham he found that the system had forgotten his existence. After more agitation for a useful occupation he was sent to London in October, 1943, for an interview that was to lead to his recruitment into SOE.

Fleming lived with his four Dutch suspects for nearly three months, after which the unfortunate Dourlein and Ubbink were thrown into Brixton prison without trial as suspected double agents, forced to associate with common criminals for two weeks until the Dutch authorities managed to extricate them. They were, Fleming reported, extremely bitter about their treatment after risking their lives to escape from Haaren to bring the news of the disaster of the SOE operations in Holland. Dourlein and Ubbink were discharged from SOE under a cloud and it was to take them five years to clear their names. Dourlein was demoted from sergeant to corporal and subsequently joined the Dutch Air Force and saw active service as an air gunner for the latter part of the war. In October, 1950, the outstanding courage of the pair was finally recognized by the Dutch government and they were awarded medals for their bravery.

Sergeant Fleming was posted to the Finishing School at Beaulieu in the spring of 1944 and served there in a multiplicity of roles. He was a Conducting Officer, rendering reports on the suitability of the student-agents under his charge, an interpreter for Nobby Clark's demonstrations in living off the land and a tutor in resistance to interrogation, while also doubling up as a Field Security sergeant in the Beaulieu area. He was destined to meet up with Jan Ubbink in Holland after the war.

The post-war investigations carried out independently by the British and Dutch authorities concluded, after a prolonged and detailed examination of the evidence, that the Germans had not managed to plant a spy within the senior ranks of SOE. Giskes, Schreieder, May and other members of the German counter-espionage team had been captured by the Allies and had been questioned for three years about their activities. Surviving Dutch agents and British and Dutch officers of the Dutch Section and other senior officers in SOE, including Colin Gubbins, had been questioned in detail and their records examined.

Both governments concluded that the British and Dutch officers controlling the Section had been negligent in failing to notice the absence of an array of security checks in the radio transmissions of agents under the Germans' control. Much of the blame fell upon the British officer who had been head of the Dutch Section during most of the period of Operation Nordpol.

Both of these high-level enquiries must have investigated how the Germans had acquired sufficient information about SOE techniques, facilities and controlling personnel to enable them to mount Nordpol, but their findings have never been released. Therefore one can only speculate about how much of this information came from the use of penetration agents and collaborators posing as reception committees, how much was disclosed freely by the captured agents and how much of it was derived from clandestine interrogation techniques.

After the war there were other examples of people being named as highly placed spies when in fact the information they had acquired had been obtained from secret sources such as code-breaking and the use of clandestine interrogation techniques. The people concerned were unable to disabuse the public because their true sources of information were still Top Secret. But that did not stop Hollywood making a film about the alleged high-level spying activities of one of them. The truth was that he had never been a spy. Throughout the war he held what soldiers called 'a soft-arsed number' in an Intelligence unit that was never put in the slightest danger, never experienced any hardship and never went anywhere near enemy territories.

Epilogue

THE BONFIRE OF MEMORIES

On 8 May, 1945, hostilities ceased in Europe. The Commandant and staff of the school issued invitations to a party at The House in the Wood to the Montagu family, to local residents and to their own relatives and friends, to celebrate the end of the war. The invitations stated that the School would be 'opening its cellars' to the guests at 9 pm.

The catering staff prepared a splendid spread of food the like of which the civilian guests had not seen since before rationing was introduced early in the war. The cellars were opened to produce wines and spirits of such a variety and quantity that the guests were left gasping with wonder as to how the School had managed to obtain it when it had all but disappeared from the normal sources of supply. Other members of the staff built a huge bonfire in the garden and topped it with an effigy of Adolf Hitler.

Soon after the guests arrived somebody started playing a piano, (one noble source said it was Paul Dehn), and staff and guests began to sing and dance. Near midnight one of the officers rang a bell for the guests to assemble round the bonfire and at midnight the Commandant, Lieutenant-Colonel Stanley Woolrych, ignited the fire and they all danced round it yelling at the tops of their voices until they collapsed with exhaustion, or with the drink, at dawn.

The bonfire was, many hoped, a bonfire of so many years of living on the brink of national and personal catastrophe, with the seemingly endless succession of bitter military defeats and set-backs and the constant threat of sudden death from enemy bullets, shells, bombs, flying bombs and ballistic missiles, with the pain and grief of bereavement and perpetual separation, from family, loved ones and friends. The relief felt by everybody exploded into uninhibited celebration, nation-wide.

According to the late the Hon. Mrs Playdell-Bourverie, it was a

142

stupendous and unforgettable binge on which to end five and a half years of warfare in Europe.

Few foresaw that the bonfire would mark the end of an era, the end of unprecedented comradeship and unselfishness and the end of a pervasive social cohesion through every section of our society, engendered by years of shared adversity. Or that the abrupt end of hostilities would leave many people stunned, and with a sudden, unexpected feeling of emptiness, incipient loneliness and bewilderment at the prospect of imminent redundancy and an uncertain future in some sort of civilian occupation in a much changed world.

Meantime the war continued in the Far East for a further three months, until August, 1945, which meant that after the VE Day party the staff of the School returned to work training agents for service in Europe and the Middle and Far East.

In June, 1945, the School was closed and disbanded and seven officers from the staff were posted to SOE in London to prepare a handbook on agent techniques.

SOE itself was rapidly disbanded and in the rush to return to normality most of its records were destroyed.

Few would have dared to predict that soon afterwards the country, and some of the officers of the School, would be sucked into another conflict with another savage and brutal political regime, communism, a conflict which became known as The Cold War.

APPENDIX A

MEMBERS OF THE STAFF OF THE FINISHING SCHOOL AT VARIOUS TIMES DURING THE WAR.

COMMANDANTS:-

Lt. Col. J.W.Munn R.A.
Lt. Col. S.H.C. Woolrych
Lt. Col. F.V. Spooner

INSTRUCTORS:-

Maj.	R.M. Brooker	Capt.	A. Drake
"	C. Skilbeck	Miss	C. Dundas. FANY
"	J. Wedgwood	Capt.	A. Enthoven
"	G.A. Hill	"	P. Follis
Capt.	H. Amies	"	G.M. Forty
"	R.H. Angelo	"	D.E.F. Green
"	D. Benn	"	J. Hackett
"	P. Boggis-Rolfe	"	T. Howard
"	H. Burgess	"	H. Hunt
"	M.W.H. Bruce	"	J. Lonsdale
"	D. Cameron	Miss	P. McFie. FANY
"	A. Campbell (Sir Alan)	Capt.	G. Morton
"	J. Childs	Mr.	H.A. Philby
"	Wm. Clark	Capt.	W.D.F. Smallwood
"	Paul Dehn	"	E.A. Sykes
"	M. Dobie	"	J. Debenham-Taylor

Capt.	H. Trefall	Capt.	J. Walker
"	D. Turberville	"	R. Walters
"	R. Vibert	"	P.B. Whitaker

HOUSE ADJUTANTS:-

Maj.	J.H.P. Barcroft
Capt.	Barry
"	R. Carr
"	W.J. Corrie
"	R.H. Harris
"	A.R. Hinde
"	F.W. Rhodes
"	P.J. Tidmarsh

ADMIN STAFF:-

Maj.	A. Wilkinson
Maj.	Palmer
Capt.	Lofts
Capt.	Parsons
A. Reith	

SECRETARIES:-

Miss Dorothy Wickens
Mrs P. Spriddell
Miss Ann Keenlyside
Miss Evadne Cull
Miss Lorna Tidmarsh
Miss Noreen Riols

FIELD SECURITY:-

L/Cpl.	B. Ettenfield
Sgt	G. Fleming
Sgt	M. Forrest
Cpl.	C.G. Holland
L/Cpl.	(later Major) R. Warden

OTHER RANKS:-

Cpl.	Don Butchers	Head Driver
Pte.	Donald	Clerk
Sgt.	Fielding	
Pte.	Jock Flockhart	Commandant's Driver
Pte.	Len Hatfield	
Q.M.S.	'Tansey' Lee	
Pte.	Morris	A.C.C.
Pte.	Purdy	A.C.C.
Pte.	Poytress	Clerk
Pte.	Jack Stacey	
L/Cpl.	Stidwell	
Cpl.	Walker	Clerk
	'Taffy' Williams.	

APPENDIX B

THE COMMANDANT'S OPENING ADDRESS TO NEW STUDENTS

AUTHOR'S NOTE:

The full text of Lieutenant-Colonel S.H.C. Woolrych's opening address to the students of many nationalities is historically interesting for a variety of reasons. It was evidently drafted sometime during 1943 when the German Army was at full stretch and the Germans were plundering the manpower of the Occupied Countries for forced labour in German industries. It also captures the spirit and the mounting tension of the Allies preparing to invade the continent of Europe and gives some inkling of the relative ease with which agents were being infiltrated into and extricated from the Occupied countries.

Compared with the sophisticated methods of today, and even in comparison with the methods of the Cold War, it reveals an astonishing naivety, and the text has a distinct flavour of the amateurism which pervaded the whole of Special Operations Executive and many of its wartime operations. It is, however, easy to be critical in retrospect, to ignore the stresses of the wartime situations. In truth they were usually such that enormous risks had to be taken by committing half-trained personnel of all Arms into action long before they were sufficiently trained to cope with the tasks they were given without risking their lives through inexperience.

Although written more than half a century ago, this address retains a contemporary ring and possesses a disagreeable familiarity in a modern world riven by warring factions, insurgency and terrorism.

THE COMMANDANT'S OPENING ADDRESS
TO NEW STUDENTS

First of all let me bid you welcome. I hope that you will enjoy your Course here and will find it helpful to you.

Now let's get to work. The purpose of the Organization to which you and I belong is Subversion. Subversion, properly applied, is one of the most potent weapons one can use. It is the fourth arm in modern warfare. What are its objects? They are fourfold. I will give you these four headings, and I would like you to pay particular attention to them as they are going to govern most of what I am going to say to you this morning.

In the first place the objective is to damage the enemy's material to the maximum extent, and also all his means of communication and production. Modern warfare is almost entirely dependent on material and communications. With every successive war there is an increasing emphasis on machines and equipment, so much so that no country without considerable industry at its call can now dream of making war on a large scale. Therefore if you destroy as many machines as possible, and damage the means of production, you have gone a long way in hampering the enemy's effort.

The second objective is to strain the enemy's resources of manpower. Towards the end of any long war the question of manpower grows every day more vital. The Germans at this moment are combing all their industries for men to put into the field, and trying to replace them with foreign labour. Every General seeks to employ the maximum amount of his resources at the vital point of attack or danger. If a sufficient force can be diverted to provide sentries, police etc. the enemy's main force is thereby weakened.

The third objective is to undermine the morale of the enemy. In any long war the question of morale becomes an increasing anxiety to leaders on both sides. If the morale of one side cracks they lose the war, however many troops they may have left. In the autumn of 1918 the German troops were no longer fighting in the same way as they had been previously. Why was that? Partly because they were getting hungrier every day, partly because they were getting tired of being kicked around by their NCOs – you can stand that on a full stomach but it is not so easy on an empty one – partly because they were getting misery letters from their people at home. The morale of the German army was cracking and, in consequence, the German army cracked. Anything we can do to help along this process during the present war is going to help to shorten it. There are plenty of methods. We must not forget also the quislings and collaborators. We want them also to feel thoroughly uncomfortable.

Finally, there is the converse of this, to raise the morale of the populations of the Occupied countries in order that they may give us vital assistance when the right moment comes.

How do we achieve all this? There are plenty of methods to produce all the effects we seek to bring about.

Damage to the enemy's material means of production is, of course, achieved by *sabotage*. Now there are various kinds of degrees of sabotage and we can put these into an ascending scale. There are at least four stages.

First of all there is the form of sabotage known as Passive Resistance – an innumerable series of small acts which entail virtually no risk to the perpetrators. The main principle is non-cooperation – making the enemy feel that, while you are keeping within the letter of his law, you are not in the least won over by him and are only waiting your chance to liberate yourselves. The enemy's life in Occupied countries should be made as thoroughly uncomfortable as possible. He should be made to feel an alien in a hostile environment. The Boche is an emotional creature who cannot stand too much dislike.

All sorts of extra work can be created for him by over-caution and especially excessive zeal. The sort of zeal that sends him anonymous denunciations of his collaborators, that sends him reports of non-existent unexploded bombs, elusive parachutists, etc. If the thing is properly worked he need never suspect that he is being made a fool of.

The second stage we may call 'industrial sabotage'. Here there is some risk to the perpetrators, but it is not excessive. In the first place anything which can be done to prevent workers going to German factories is all to the good. As we have said, the Boche is anxious to recruit all the foreign labour he can in order to release his own men for the Army. Let us try to stop that. But one may well take advantage of the fact that the workers will undoubtedly continue to flock to Germany, whether as volunteers or as conscripts, by including amongst them agents recruited specially for the purpose of starting sabotage in German factories. Here the possibilities are immense. The Germans claim to have already dispatched millions of foreign workers to Germany and only a very small percentage of these workers can really wish Germany to win the war.

In the third place, a great deal of damage can be done in factories and workshops by omitting to carry out certain essential functions, such as lubricating, or by substituting some abrasive for the real lubricant.

Lastly, workers can also hold up German production by a measurable percentage by causing waste and delay, and by excessive zeal or by over-caution. One can insist upon pedantic adherence to regulations or ask for frequent renewals and overhauls of machinery 'so as to produce the best results'. Too much time can be spent on doing any one job. One can always appear to insist upon an unnecessarily high standard. If every worker in every German factory were to leave his bench for the purposes of nature for double the usual period, the effect on production would be quite measurable. One can also waste precious lubricants by over-lubrication, and time by too much attention to the safety regulations.

The third stage of sabotage might be called 'minor sabotage', that is, isolated acts of definite destruction, such as blowing up a bridge, an electric transformer, wrecking power lines, etc. These do, of course, entail very considerable risk to the perpetrators but they have a definite nuisance value.

Lastly we come to sabotage on a grand scale – 'major sabotage', let's call it. This might involve the destruction of whole lengths of railway, bridges and roads in a given area. Naturally there can be no attempt at concealment of these once they have occurred, although they would, naturally, be prepared under extremely secret conditions. They can only be accomplished by organized saboteur squads and they would be timed to coincide with some big event, such as invasion. So much for sabotage.

Now is this all that sabotage can accomplish? No. Successful sabotage also has the effect of straining the enemy's resources of manpower. This is effected in at least two different ways. All this faulty workmanship in factories which we have detailed needs putting right. It is not merely a question of duplicating labour – it may be far worse than that – a definite damage to the machine may have occurred by this careless lack of lubrication, for instance. Every attack which is made on rolling stock, and especially locomotives, must be the very devil for the enemy's repair shops which are already congested. In this way the enemy's resources of civilian manpower are being wasted.

149

But there is another aspect as well. Whenever a major act of sabotage occurs, the Gestapo swarm all over the district to make enquiries, and they nearly always result in recommendations for increased guards on these or other points. The more extra sentries we can get posted at points we do not intend to attack the better. If we can get whole police battalions diverted to certain areas it is better still.

How do we set about undermining the morale of enemy troops? Well, there are several methods of political subversion about which you will get details during the next few weeks. It is no good trying to plant downright falsehoods on enemy troops; you have no right to expect them to swallow them. But you *can* work on grievances which they already have. You can fan their dissatisfaction with their conditions, and also the anxiety they must feel for their relations in North German towns which have been heavily blitzed by the RAF. You can play on the feeling of loneliness some of their troops must experience in remote stations, and on the terror they must feel at the risk of being stabbed in the back by the population they are holding in check when 'the day' arrives. And you can make them almost sob at the thought of all they are being deprived of.

Lastly, you can raise the morale of the population of the occupied countries by various forms of propaganda which are being used at this moment in every German Occupied country every day of the year. The object of this propaganda is to unify the population in a common hatred of the Boche. Arising out of this there should come the sort of non-cooperation with him which is so important to us. One can implant in them the conviction amounting to certainty that the Allies will win – from that should spring an active desire to help that victory forward.

These, then, are the objects which we seek to attain by subversion, and I have just detailed some of the methods by which they can be achieved. It is obvious, however, that all these effects will be haphazard and therefore largely wasted if they are not all bound up in a general plan which covers all activities, and times them all to fit, like a railway schedule. Each single act of sabotage, or propaganda, or political subversion ought to be part of a definite plan of attack.

The plan naturally varies with each country and there are several factors which govern it. There is first of all, naturally, military strategy, for all our subversive efforts are governed by what the main plan of attack may be – and subversion is only one part of a very large whole. It is no use, for instance, laying on an ambitious plan of sabotage for a country which the High Command has decided at the last moment not to attack – unless it is a deliberate plan of diversion.

It is naturally also influenced by the German economic situation. For instance, one of the main German weaknesses at the moment is communications, and that is why they are so constantly attacked both by RAF bombers and saboteurs. Then there is the question of the political situation. The relations between the Allies and some so-called neutral countries are so delicate that no subversive operations can be contemplated in those countries for the time being, even though it is apparent that they may be next on the list for attack by the Germans. There is also the nature of the country to be considered – the density of its population and the degree of industrialization. It is obvious that the plan for small, densely populated and highly industrialized countries such as Belgium and Holland would be different from the deserts of Libya – if there is one.

Lastly the attitude of the civilian population may make a considerable difference to the plan. In some countries secret organizations already exist in fairly large numbers and they may have to be taken into consideration. The attitude of some Occupied countries is far more virile than that of others, who are inclined to lie down and do nothing about it. In some parts of the country there may even be an active pro-Nazi element. All these factors have to be weighed.

The general policy in whatever country you may be sent to can be divided into two phases – the pre-invasion phase and the invasion phase. Let us take the pre-invasion phase first.

The first essential is to organize each country, area by area. Naturally the organization in each country will vary enormously according to factors of geography, population and industry, so that no two countries will be entirely alike. For the same reasons the organization inside each area may be extremely simple or, on the other hand, it may be a fairly complex organization closely knit together. In addition to the factors I have already mentioned, there is the dominating factor of the German C.E. (Counter-Espionage) control. It is their activities which mostly dictate what kind of organization one can stage. Then there is the question of the native organizations already working inside the country – the so-called secret armies. Here again the policy varies so much from country to country and according to the run of the war, that it is impossible to lay down any universal principle. In some countries organizers may be asked to go out as pioneers and organize guerrilla bands with various objectives to be attacked when the 'day' comes. In other countries agents are sent out regularly to form part of the powerful secret organizations already existing, and to fill niches in those organizations, such as arms instructors, sub-area organizers, W/T operators etc. Yet in other

151

countries, the organization of which you form a part functions entirely separately from these organizations, which are probably too well known to the Boche. But even in these cases some attempt must be made to take note of these local societies and to assess their value.

Naturally most of your activities will form a preparation for the great day when your countries come to be liberated and the invasion phase should, therefore, see your activities at maximum stretch. Everything depends upon the secrecy and efficiency with which the preparations are made. The more that each separate operation can be prepared, and even possibly, rehearsed, the better it is likely to go off when the day comes.

Here again the operational orders naturally vary considerably for each country, so that it is impossible to lay down any universal plan to apply to all countries. Nevertheless, the activities some part of which you will probably be asked to prepare for, will include such things as:-

a) A whole series of combined attacks on the enemy's rail, road and telecommunications, if, for instance, it were possible to isolate completely for even 48 hours, a vital strategic centre 50 miles behind the enemy's lines just at the moment when the Allies were landing, just think of the gift this would be to the Allied commander. If it were impossible for the enemy to get his troops up to the threatened spot at the right moment because his communications were temporarily sabotaged, it might make all the difference to the success or failure of the operations – in that sector at all events.

b) Demolishing important river bridges which are vital to the enemy's communications. Or, conversely, preventing the enemy from doing so when he wishes to prevent the Allies from advancing. The campaign of 1940 in the Low Countries showed what tragic results to the defence can result from a single important bridge failing to be demolished. And it is about time that the Germans had some of their own medicine.

c) Attacks on enemy HQ's, telephone installations, wireless vans etc. A small gang of disciplined men can very soon deal with even an important enemy HQ if the operation is thoroughly studied and planned beforehand. If the sentries are attacked at exactly the right moment and the men in the guardroom are overwhelmed, one can very soon overrun the whole HQ building by running down the corridors and throwing bombs or grenades into each room. They are fairly effective weapons in those conditions.

d) Blocking roads which must be used by the enemy's transport but care must be taken not to block roads which may be required by the advancing Allies. It has been rightly pointed out that it is impossible to block any road for more than a certain time. Nevertheless if the enemy had to vacate a town at a moment's notice, with a large amount of transport, and then have to deal with road blocks, or possibly road craters, it might make all the difference to them, more especially if the sky was filled with bombing aeroplanes which leave them no respite.

e) The question of the civil population is a very important one, for it was their action in pouring out on to all the roads before the advancing Germans in 1940 that seriously handicapped the Allies in their attempts to deal with the German invasion. Here again detailed plans will be worked out in due course to tell the civil population what they can do to help, and especially what they can avoid doing to hinder. No doubt the BBC will play a large part in this, but one cannot rely on the civilian population having receivers in an area threatened by invasion, and it may well be that your services may prove extremely useful in coping with an urgent problem of this kind.

Where does the organizer fit into all these schemes? The organizer is the key man in all of them and it is on his work and organization that the smooth carrying out of all the plans depends. You will have seen enough from what I have told you to realize that any one organizer has only a very small part – although an important one – in a vast organization, and that any work he carries out is only a minute part of a big general plan. You will therefore appreciate the absolute necessity of team work. Too much individualism on the part of any one organizer might go far to wreck the plan.

The roles of the organizer are various. More often than not he is sent into the field with a specific mission to carry out. He may be given a target to demolish; he may be asked to ferment industrial unrest in a particular area; he may be asked to organize a small guerrilla band in a certain district. On the other hand he may be sent out as a pioneer with instructions to organize a certain area. In that case he starts from scratch. He will have to make a survey of his area, and decide what are the most suitable targets to attack, and what type of organization is best adapted to the purpose. If he is working not far from this country, and is in fairly close touch, he will probably report back either by W/T or by letter, or, more likely still, return on a short visit. On the other hand, if the spot to which he goes is at the other end of the earth, we may not see him back again before the end of the war and he will have to use his own initiative throughout.

It is obvious he can do none of these things unless he is properly trained and equipped for his task. That is why you have come to Beaulieu. During the next few weeks you will have the task of studying the underground life in every aspect – starting with the moment at which you arrive on the ground and disengage yourself from your parachute. You will have to learn to bury it safely, and to start your new life in your new surround-ings. We shall be discussing with you every kind of measures for your own safety – the importance of having the right story to tell, the right kind of job to do, and how to lead your life best in accordance with those facts. We shall teach you how to build up your organization from zero. There is only one word of warning I wish to make here. If you follow conscien-tiously in the field all that we teach you here, we cannot guarantee your safety, but we think that your chance of being picked up is very small. Remember, the best agents are never caught. But some agents when they get out into the field find it apparently much easier than they expected, and they are inclined to relax their precautions. That is the moment to beware of. Never relax your precautions, and never fool yourself by thinking that the enemy are asleep. They may be watching you all the time, so watch your step.

BIBLIOGRAPHY

Amies, Hardie	*Just So Far*	1954	Collins
Andrew, C.	*Secret Service*	1985	Sceptre
Braddon, Russell	*Nancy Wake*	1956	The Book Club
Buckmaster, M.	*They Fought Alone*	1958	Odhams Press
Buckmaster, M.	*Specially Employed*	1952	Batchworth
Butler, Ewan	*Amateur Agent*	1963	Harrap
Bruce, Lockhart, R.	*Ace of Spies*	1967	Hodder & Stoughton
Churchill, Peter	*Of Their Own Choice*	1952	Hodder & Stoughton
Churchill, Winston	*The Second World War*	1952	Cassell & Co.
Clayton, Anthony	*Forearmed*	1993	Brassey's
Cowles, V.	*Phantom Major*	1958	Companion Book Club
Dourlein, P.	*Inside North Pole*	1953	Wm. Kimber
Fiocca, Nancy	*The White Mouse*	1985	Macmillan
Foot, M.R.D.	*S.O.E. in France*	1966	HMSO
Foot, M.R.D.	*S.O.E. 1940–46*	1984	B.B.C. Publication
Foot, M.R.D. and Langley, J.M.	*M.I.9.*	1979	Book Club Associates
Garlinski, J.	*Poland, SOE and the Allies*	1969	Allen & Unwin
Giskes, H.J.	*London Calling North Pole*	1953	Wm. Kimber
Haswell, J.	*British Military Intelligence*	1973	Weidenfeld & Nicolson
Haukelid, Knut	*Skis Against the Atom*	1954	Wm. Kimber

Howarth, P.	*Undercover*	1980	Routledge & Kegan Paul
Howe, E.	*The Black Game*	1982	Michael Joseph
Jones, Liame	*A Quiet Courage*	1991	Corgi
Jones, R.V.	*Most Secret War*	1978	Hodder & Stoughton
King, Stella	*Jacqueline*	1989	Arms & Armour
Knightly, P.	*Philby KGB Masterspy*	1988	Andre Deutsch
Marshall, Bruce	*White Rabbit*	1952	Evans
MacDonald, C.	*The Killing of Obergruppenführer Heydrich*	1989	Macmillan
Maclean, Fitzroy	*Eastern Approaches*	1949	Jonathan Cape
Messenger, Charles	*The Commandos*	1991	Grafton Books
Minney, R.J.	*Carve her Name with Pride*	1956	George Newnes
Philby, Kim	*My Silent War*	1963	Harrap
Piquet-Wicks, E.	*Four in the Shadows*	1957	Jarrolds
Stafford, David	*Camp X*	1986	Viking
Sweet-Escott, B.	*Baker St. Irregular*	1965	Methuen & Co.
West, Nigel	*M.I.5.*	1983	Triad/ Panther
West, Nigel	*M.I.6.*	1983	Weidenfeld & Nicolson
Vibert, R.	*Memoirs of a Jerseyman*	1991	La Haule Books
Wilkinson and Astley	*Gubbins and SOE*	1993	Leo Cooper

INDEX

There are separate indexes for Personnel, Organizations, Topics and Places